A House
in the
High Hills

A House in the High Hills

Selina Scott

EBURY
PRESS

1 3 5 7 9 10 8 6 4 2

This edition published 2010
First published in 2009 by as *A Long Walk in the High Hills*
by Ebury Press, an imprint of Ebury Publishing
A Random House Group company

The Random House Group Limited Reg. No. 954009

Addresses for companies within the Random House Group can be
found at www.randomhouse.co.uk

A CIP catalogue record for this book is available from the British Library

The Random House Group Limited supports The Forest Stewardship
Council (FSC), the leading international forest certification organisation.
All our titles that are printed on Greenpeace approved FSC certified
paper carry the FSC logo. Our paper procurement policy
can be found at www.rbooks.co.uk/environment

Mixed Sources
Product group from well-managed
forests and other controlled sources
www.fsc.org Cert no. TT-COC-2139
FSC © 1996 Forest Stewardship Council

Printed in the UK by CPI Cox & Wyman, Reading, RG1 8EX

ISBN 9780091914479

To buy books by your favourite authors and register for offers visit
www.rbooks.co.uk

For my father, whose encouragement, sense of humour and love of all things Mallorquín made this book possible

This is a true story but, where appropriate, some names, personal details, geography and chronology have been altered to help preserve the anonymity of those involved.

Introduction

I guess it was the smudges under my eyes that sparked my first encounter with Mallorca. What I needed was a blissful week in the sun, a break from a regime of rising at three in the morning back in Britain.

I was the first woman to anchor BBC's *Breakfast Time*, a concept so innovative every squeak, it seemed, had to be recorded by a competitive tabloid press hungry for the slightest slip. Each day I'd wake to find my face, my every move, plastered over almost every newspaper across the nation. It was part of the job, of course, but even so it wasn't tremendous fun and then a friend in the fashion business noticed the dark circles and the way I gravitated to wearing frocks of black and grey on the show and phoned to offer me sunshine. She and her husband had a house in Spain, not wanting to admit, at first, it was Mallorca, and 'it's yours for as long as you need it', she told me. I glanced in the mirror and a month later I was heading to the Balearics.

Mallorca has a strange smell in high summer. Like cat pee. It clobbers you the moment the plane lands and the doors open. It's a herb, apparently, whose pheromones are released under intense heat. So this was okay, I told myself on that first visit. A bit of warmth might do the same for me and, anyway, I didn't intend to stay for long. I had never really fancied Mallorca, imagining a package holiday kind of place with high-rises on wrecked beaches; bus trips, fish and chips and jolly Brits packing pubs all along the coast from Magaluff to Palma Nova.

My first night on the island, however, was revelatory. A clear dark sky pierced with stars, sheep bells tinkling in the hills and the scent of wild lavender, jasmine and thyme coating the warm enveloping air with exotic sweetness. I was still waking early, hardly believing that instead of a dingy trip in a dark cab to an old tram shed (Lime Grove) in West London where the BBC celebrates its *Breakfast*, I was gladly greeting a different dawn in a quiet Mallorquín village. From my friend's house the view over the valley to the distant hills was almost medieval; nothing stirred as cockbirds began calling one another through a fragile morning mist.

Unable to resist, I set off in the coolness to walk to the coast about three miles away, guessing if I followed an old cart track at the edge of the village I would miss the main road and find my way through the pine trees to the fishing port of San Telm. Then I could leap into the Mediterranean and swim and swim.

The track began gently, winding through a cluster of whitewashed village houses where fat black grapes draped over each backyard before veering off, getting steeper, leading up through a rocky gully. As I began to climb, a flash of brilliance, a hoopoe bird suddenly darted out of a bush, racing ahead, beating me to the top. I just caught its brightness as it descended into a valley of almond and olive trees in the middle of which sat an ancient farmhouse.

The place was deserted. Intrigued, I stepped off the path, wading through a field knee high with wild fennel to take a closer look. At the front of the house an old vine propped on a gnarled branch of holm oak, sprawled across canes, offering shade, sheltering a simple wooden table and a couple of stick chairs. A gaudy splash of purple bougainvillea clung to the periphery, struggling. All around were old stone walls, beginning to slip.

The shuttered house had two arched doors, made of massive pine planks whose primitive nails and blackened ringed handles gave the place an air of working antiquity. A stone bread oven, perfectly crafted and still in use, leaned against the side of the house, its smooth floor at waist height. The oven must have baked a mountain of bread over the years. I was so absorbed in the peace of this early Mediterranean morning that a raucous squawk from the hoopoe as it rocketed out of the bougainvillea startled me. I suddenly realised I was a little too close to someone's home in this completely unexpected pocket of Mallorca. Any minute whoever owned this place might turn up and find me. Reluctantly I left.

That brief holiday spent in the sun and sea of Mallorca was the beginning, luring me to look again. A few months later and I was back, to meet an English couple who owned the farmhouse in the enchanting valley. I'd been told they had to sell because they needed to return to the UK, so on impulse I agreed to see them, with no intention, of course, of actually making an offer. It was March, a damp, grey day in Britain when I reacquainted myself with the island having been warned by all those who knew me well that to take on a project like this was madness when I was so immersed in TV.

Sheila and Johnny were waiting, sitting at the old table under the makeshift pergola when I showed up, desultorily proffering a glass of rain water from an old earthenware jug. Obviously I wasn't what they considered a serious contender. The water tasted peculiar.

Sheila and Johnny were middle-aged and also, it struck me, a little defeated. While Johnny untangled a strand of stray tobacco from his pipe it was left to Sheila, slim and blonde and slightly defensive, to make a tentative sales pitch as a shaft of sun caught a spider in mid-spin tumbling from the vine above.

Would I like to see the house? Of course. Sheila got up and walked to the arched front door. Pushing hard, the door swung with a creak against a whitewashed wall to reveal an enormous quarry-tiled room, where a traditional Mallorquín fireplace took up a whole corner. I had never seen anything like it. Its massive canopy constructed from cane and horse-hair plaster was supported by a large branch of olive. Under its embrace whole families would congregate to eat and cook and keep warm in winter. It was remarkable that it had survived so long.

Next door was another large room. It too had a corner fire-place, framed with hanging bundles of dried herbs. Sheila had collected English chairs and pictures, which had been haphaz-ardly arranged around the rough walls. From the ground floor, a steep tiled staircase divided the house in two and led to bedrooms under the eaves. The bathroom was downstairs attached to the house with a low sloping roof.

It was all very simple and basic but when I admired it she told me the house was about two hundred years old, built by the family who once owned the entire valley. Sheila and Johnny had bought it many years back, when it had long been empty, restoring it with the little money they had, but there was still much that needed doing, she said.

We stood in silence, contemplating just how much needed to be done as dust rose, rallying in the air. Johnny came into the room, settling into what I took to be his favourite sofa covered in tartan throws under the window as I perched in my pretty frock on an upright chair opposite. Did I realise, he said, that there isn't any electricity here? Johnny chewed at his pipe, gazing at the wet end of it as he extracted it from his lips. My eyes rested on the porcelain shades above the wall lights. 'We run everything on gas which comes in bottles which have to be carried from the village,' he continued, 'and our only other source of power is...' he paused. I felt oddly unsuited for what was coming next. 'A genny,' he announced. 'It's in the dunny.' The dunny.

We all trooped outside, to the remnants of an old pig sty. It was filled with Johnny's tools and petrol cans and right at the back there it was: the genny. I peered into the gloom not realising then that this thing would be the first in a long line of temperamental generators that would test me and my sunny nature to the limit.

At that moment, the three of us in silence outside the dunny, Johnny rightly decided I was a no-hoper. If I couldn't show enthusiasm for his genny, his most essential bit of kit, how could I possibly begin to cope with this piece of hard work in the sun? I felt what little interest he had in me as a prospective buyer suddenly drain away. Sheila, however, was not for giving up so easily. Her hopes rose when she realised I hadn't quite clocked the water problem. I believed her when she told me a water tanker came with fresh spring water to fill up the 'deposito', an underground concrete construction at the back of the house. Certainly, I had seen the tanker doing its rounds in the village but of course she wasn't about to tell me that the road was so bad the tanker had pretty much given up on them and instead they relied on a kindly Mallorquín with a tractor dragging a water bowser behind him.

We had pretty much come to the end of our conversation

when into the field in front of the house trotted a mule and a plough. Attached to the plough was a chunky fellow with a mass of golden curls. 'Oh, that's Gunther,' Sheila announced. 'He's our neighbour. We let him have access across our fields so the drilling machine, which was too big to negotiate his road, could bore for water. In return, he's promised us a supply if ever we need it. You won't be stuck.' She pointed to a black polythene pipe that reared defiantly out of the hedge. It had been cut off. Someone had bent the pipe back and tied it with string to stop what I guessed must be water leaking out. It lay floppily within walking distance, tantalisingly close. I was idly wondering why Gunther hadn't brought the pipe right up to the house when the braying mule rounded the corner. Sheila and Johnny glanced at one another, bracing themselves, it seemed, for an encounter they hadn't anticipated.

Close up Gunther must have been in his fifties, with clear blue eyes and a smile like a car crash. Gunther was from Dusseldorf and spoke English fluently, if a little erratically. He had apparently arrived on the island after the war and had settled into an old farmstead further up the valley with his partner Francine at around the same time as Johnny and Sheila. After the usual introductions, Gunther's first words to me were: 'I know Sheila and Johnny. I don't know you. I am not giving you any water.'

It puzzled me why Gunther found it necessary to burst in with his welcoming words when Sheila and Johnny were so desperate to sell, but as I was to later discover, this was

Gunther being Gunther at his best. The truth was, at that moment I had as much desire to know this man as he had to know me.

I'd come to Mallorca again out of curiosity, to perhaps find somewhere that might allow me to evade prying eyes and get away from the demands of a high-profile television career. I was not interested in neighbourly inquisitiveness, and Gunther not showing any only added to the appeal of the place. As Sheila and Johnny squirmed beside me and Gunther stood square with his hands in his dungarees, I made up my mind.

If these three could live here full time without electricity why couldn't I? The more basic the better, as far as I was concerned. It was to be my hideaway, a downbeat to the frenetic. And anyway, candles are romantic, aren't they? Sheila and Johnny couldn't envisage their old age in the valley and wanted to return to the UK; I needed to make my escape from Britain when I wanted. I hadn't been desperately looking for a home in the sun but suddenly I was on the verge of buying one. In the gentle air of a March morning, the deal was almost done.

It fell to a sombre lawyer in Palma to actually close it. His office was up three flights of stairs in a back street of the city, a slumbering city then, which shut down at three in the afternoon and did business in the morning and early evening hours behind the most grandiose of doors, it seemed to me, in the most palatial of buildings. The wealth brought to Mallorca over the centuries by mercantile activity under both the Arabs and Christians was still discernible in the decaying mansions, and distressed magnificent churches packed tight in its city centre. What was pleasing about Palma was its diversity and colour. Its poor had not yet been siphoned off to the outskirts, their apartments in the older streets had grass in the gutters, peeling paintwork and washing hung in tiers from once glamorous, wrought-iron balconies. Commerce rubbed up against near destitution, so a walk through the city had a frisson, window-shopping one minute, a little on alert the next. Glitz traded alongside gypsies, down-and-outs, drug dealers and prostitutes. Palma was like a faded, expressionistic Spanish work of art.

Straight out of an El Greco was Luis Rodriguez. A small brass plate above a great brass doorknob announced my lawyer who spoke not a word of English and I no Spanish that made any sense to him. Luis had straight, black hair, swept high off his head, which gave him an oddly elongated appearance. Luis spoke slowly to me at first, out of politeness that I might understand better the maze I was about to enter. 'Señora Selina, *comprende*?'

'Er, *un poco.*'

In this courteous manner we conducted our mighty affair of purchasing the property for what seemed like months.

Finally, the day came when I took possession of the house, but it was a day I would never wish to repeat. Marching from Luis's office to a *notario* in a downtown backstreet to file final papers I didn't have a clue about nearly broke my resolve. The one unpalatable fact I had managed to grasp was that although I paid the full asking price for the house this wasn't the figure that was going to be put in the Escritura. A tiny sum had to be entered for the benefit of the sellers, normal practice in those days. It meant Johnny and Sheila wouldn't have to pay a large tax bill. I didn't have the words to instruct Luis to do otherwise. That was the way it worked in Spain. And that was that. There was now no turning back.

one

Something clatters on the roof, falling and bouncing down the tiles. It is hot. A humid heat on an August night, my first in a ruined house in a secluded valley in the south-west corner of Mallorca I so recklessly decided would be perfect for me just six months before. The noise above my bed gains speed and volume. It's obviously an animal of some kind – the kind I don't want to contemplate. Rats? What else comes out to play on a steaming Mediterranean night? I pull the mosquito net closer and hope that whatever it is won't hop in through the open window as I eventually, somehow, manage to drift off to sleep.

I am awake. Whatever had been hammering on the roof overnight has gone. The grey morning light encourages me to rise before the cicadas begin to saw in the pines close by. The heat won't be here for another hour or more so there is just time to sweep the thick stone slabs at the front of the house and wash my T-shirts and shorts, which will be dry before noon. I manage to rig up a mirror from a box shipped from Britain, hang it on a prickly branch of pomegranate and, with warm water in an old enamel bowl, bathe in the open air.

Life suddenly seems easy on this August morning even though I still have a pile of furniture to sort out. Sheila and Johnny had scarpered with all theirs, leaving me only the genny 'on loan' and, in the bathroom downstairs, three bulky orange gas bottles lined up like bouncers outside a nightclub.

Standing in the sun, however, under the pomegranate tree, I'm in no hurry. It can all wait. Yesterday had been a marathon. I'd hired a massive pantechnicon back home and filled it with what essential household gear I could muster. It had then set off, trundling across Europe to rendezvous with a smaller van at the bottom of the track which then ferried the lot in little loads up to the house. It had taken all day in blistering heat, but by night I was fully installed with a wad of paperwork – an inventory that catalogued knives, forks, a pot hoopoe bird made into a lamp that a friend had given me as a joke… the list ran to six pages which would have to be sent to immigration along with a deposit, refunded to me three years down the line. Don't for one minute ask me why.

Now all I want is to take a walk, perhaps to the village to pick up some fresh bread and enjoy the day before it gets too hot. The walk won't take long, the village is about a mile down the road, in a bowl of almond and olive orchards sheltered all round by the pine-clad hills of the Sierra Tramuntana. From the backstreets of the village more tracks lead up and on to the high plateau, footpaths into a wilder landscape of dramatic cliffs and soaring hawks. When the rains fall here racing down the mountain slopes, '*torrentes*', deep man-made gulleys, catch and funnel the floods before they reach the village, channelling them straight out to sea. In the dry months, the village's *torrente* sprouts clumps of cane and masses of bright blue morning glory, a secret hiding place for feral cats only a few paw prints from the main street, which runs east to west. Three grocery shops, a butcher, an iron-monger, two bakers, two banks, a carpenter, a tobacconist, an electrician, a post office, a hairdresser, a primary school, a garage and two bars march along its length.

The village was once situated higher up the valley but drought in the eighteenth century forced families down into lower-lying land where wells could more easily be dug to catch springs. It must have been extremely tough for the people who lived here then. At the turn of the twentieth century, years of uncertainty and near starvation during a series of desiccated harvests led whole families to leave the island and find their fortunes in Cuba or France. Those who returned from Nantes with fortunes made from growing and selling vegetables built grand, art deco homes with cupolas, four storeys high to catch whatever breeze was blowing.

They renamed the main street 'the road of the French', in memory of their exile, an architectural wonder today, although more modest two-storey dwellings like the local bar must have been here many years before. On my first morning in my new house I head to this bar, Sancho's, for what will become a life-time addiction to strong coffee.

Sancho and his wife Pepita throw open their bright green shutters early each morning, carrying out tables and chairs to arrange under the geraniums flowering in the window, cram-ming the narrow pavement in front. The bar doesn't close until the last customer leaves. Keeping count of these long hours across the road is the old church clock whose bell marks every quarter hour, half hour and hour twice over with the loudest gong. I guess the folk living nearby are used to it, for this clock doesn't differentiate between night and day, insist-ing on doing double duty when most are thinking of their beds, hitting midnight with twenty-four sleep-busting bangs. This idiosyncratic way of telling villagers the time started in the years when most were out working in the fields. It was a resounding reminder of the hour if, for some reason, they missed the chimes the first time round.

The coffee machine in Sancho's hisses and gurgles through the day, first for the workmen who pop in to have a cognac or a *cana* (a beer) and then for the more leisurely, the artists and writers, who arrive later in the day from homes scattered round the district to catch up on local news before picking up groceries or newspapers from one of the three *colmadas*, tiny grocery shops hidden within the back alleys of the village.

Sancho seems to have a perpetual twinkle which hits high octane whenever he spies an attractive woman. For some reason he is forever chewing a matchstick which is permanently clamped between his front teeth. '*¿Que tal?*' How are you today, Sancho? He might respond, '*¡Magnifico!*' or maybe, if I am lucky, '*¡Musculo!*', bending his elbow to show how strong a fellow he truly is. A gigantic wink always comes as part of the deal. Sancho was born in Soller in the north of the island where all the oranges and lemons grow and when you talk to him about this place, his eyes mist over. Today he is voluble about a couple of trees being planted by the council, in a nearby cul-de-sac. A woman is telling him how the greenery will enhance the village, but Sancho is having none of it. '*Problemas, muchas problemas,*' he says, shaking his head. The foliage is only going to encourage youngsters to hide and get up to mischief. Sancho is knowledgeable about things like this because he was once a cop in Barcelona.

His bar is just one room deep and has eight marble tables with chairs. There are several black-and-white sketches and watercolours from appreciative clients on the walls, including one, incongruously, of a river scene in Wales along with a list of forthcoming fiestas. A large fan whirs overhead. At the back of the bar, close to the stairs leading to Sancho and Pepita's living quarters above, is a table where mail is left. The bar acts as a kind of dead letter drop, post being easier to leave here than deliver to houses at the end of goat tracks in the district. Which means everyone knows who's up to what. The overspill from the post table often ends up on the stairs wedged between bottles and cartons waiting to be ferried out to crates in the back garden. There is always a lot of rummaging going on at the back of the bar.

A tiny window above the post table opens to a spectacular view of the mountains but the regulars here aren't into appreciation of the landscape this early in the morning, there are more pressing concerns. Like shouting at one another. Above the noise of happy chatter I manage to order a black coffee and an ensaimada (a local speciality, a yeast pastry twirled into a flat bun and drizzled with icing sugar), as Sancho dives into his sweety jar to dispense goodies to the little ones who have come into the bar that morning with their parents. From the takings of this small enterprise Sancho and Pepita have raised a family: two girls, Pia and Sofia, and a son, Paco, all now grown. My café Americano hits the spot.

I've squeezed into a corner table in the window to get a better view of early morning village life and am beginning to feel slightly disorientated. My breakfast routine of rising at three to shine on live TV back in Britain is beginning to kick in, my mind at this hour in the morning racing. I have been coming round to thinking that now might be time to try something fresh, to reconnect with a grown-up world away from *Breakfast* on the BBC, but embracing a less hectic rhythm is obviously not going to be easy. Perhaps my immersion in a ruin in Mallorca in high summer will nudge me towards change ever so gradually and give me perspective on where my career might lead.

———

Certainly, as each day passes I'm discovering something new around me. I hadn't counted, for example, the scattering of almond trees in front of my house, until now. There are twenty. Some as thick as an oak, others just tiny sprigs, their leaves wilting in the heat. Dozens of wild olive trees race along the boundaries and here and there stand overburdened fig trees, desperate to deliver their bonanza of juicy black fruit. Wading through the tall dry grasses towards the house, clutching my *barra* of fresh bread from the village, I am struck, again, by how remarkable are the gnarled, old fruit trees, aligned a few steps from the front door still giving shade and sustenance. To have them survive until now is a blessing. What is particularly pleasing is the ancient plum, its great crown bent over, like an umbrella, shaped as if to protect the house from the sun but of course it has positioned itself for a ripening.

This morning I wish I could lie out under its shade but a rattle from a generator has erupted further up the valley, quickly followed by another, calling me to join the chorus. I can see it's addictive, this noise pollution, because it's vital to existence here. Without an active generator I won't have running water in the house, so Johnny's genny, lurking in the darkness of the dunny, will have to be tackled. Once that's licked I can plug in a cable, which will power the submersible pump in the *cisterna* to lift rain water up to a tank in one of the front bedrooms where it'll tumble by gravity to the kitchen and bathroom below. It all sounds complicated but I've been assured it is very straightforward.

First, though, the *cisterna* needs checking. It's onion-shaped, a massive black hole at the front of the house, dug centuries back to catch every available drop of rain from the roof. A big iron key hanging on a board inside the house opens the *cisterna*'s olive wood door for me to lean in and check the water level. Down in the blackness, the *cisterna* harbours what look like the tentacles of a giant squid but are in fact the whitened, tangled roots of the vine which has pushed through the clay lining into the depths to draw in vital moisture. It's all a bit creepy but through the gloom I'm relieved to see I have enough rain water to last a few more weeks.

It's surprising how much water one person can use when it is hot. And of course, in August, there is usually no rain. Hardly a drop falls in summer but with plenty of water underground I can relax. I won't have to engage just yet with the water tanker and the *deposito*.

The *deposito* is another of Johnny's contraptions skulking at the back of the house under the brambles. It acts as a backup supply to the *cisterna* and has a heavy lid with a bit of electrical cord attached to help lift it for a quick inspection. The *deposito* is where the water tanker, if it can make it up the track, drops its load.

The cacophony of generators in the valley must have been

running for over an hour now so I can't put it off any longer. I have to grapple with the genny in the dunny but as soon as I attempt to coax it into action it does what I guessed it would: rebel. No matter how much I pull the cord to catch a rev I get no joy. Have I overdone it on the choke? I decide to wait to let it cool or de-coke or whatever it has to do. I mustn't panic: I have to conquer this misery-guts of a machine because the two of us are in this bind together.

Finally, after about ten minutes and a lot of spluttering, the genny hits its stride. I adjust the choke lever and let the machine run, clattering along with its neighbour for another hour until mine finally runs out of fuel and dies. But I'm ready for it. Like an alchemist, I have a row of different polythene containers lined up ready for action. A sticky bottle of pinky-red oil, a five-gallon drum of petrol and another to mix the two together. Hey presto, two-stroke. After the genny's gone off the boil, I'm back in business.

Thankfully, powering the house with light and heat is an altogether more sophisticated affair. Every Tuesday a clanking wagon reels into town giddy with the weight of a hundred bottles of gas. If I'm there to meet it, I can exchange my empties for full for a few pesetas but even empty bottles weigh mightily and full ones can lay a girl out cold. The drill, apparently, is to deposit empties the night before at Sancho's because his muscular son, Paco, will help lift the refills into the back of a car the next morning. A full bottle of gas is a killer no matter how I look at it. And I'm going to need three of the brutes a week. One will be hooked to the fridge, another to the hot-water boiler, and the third to the gaslights in the sitting room. If I run out of gas for lights it's back to candles.

It's only when I relate the dos and don'ts of power and light and water to friends who want to stay that I come over all shaky. Everyone, it seems, thinks it's ridiculous that I have gone and bought a house with no running water or electricity. The house has a telephone line but that's about it. What was I thinking? I can't think of a good explanation either. It all sounds too potty for words. The price of solitude, well, not for long anyway.

As I step into the coolness of the stone house, my eyes adjusting to the dark, the phone begins to ring. I have only been on the island a couple of days and already I'm being asked to leave. It is CBS in America, calling to firm up a meeting in London to talk about a new show launching in New York. It sounds interesting. They want to pitch a proposal to me but unluckily my trip will coincide with a visit friends of mine have already booked with their children. Now they'll have to cope on their own.

The next few days are spent in a hot fug of activity. The weather has turned sultry and getting the house into shape quicker than I had planned is proving wearisome. Happily, however, I've discovered the second bar in the village, the one run by Lorenzo and his pretty wife Beatriz, along with Lorenzo's mother and father. It is set back at an angle from the main street which lends it an exclusive air. It's also a bit quieter than Sancho's, and calmer. Perfect for me just now.

Lorenzo roars off most mornings on his motor scooter, a cigar welded to his lips, his helmet askew, to deliver newspapers in San Telm, or at least that's his excuse. It seems to me this job is simply a way of catching up on cheery happenings over the hill, stopping off at the many bars along the seafront to get the gossip. Lorenzo is a robust, imposing chap who, like a lot of Spanish men, appears bemused at being so doted on by the women in his life. He effects an air of patrimony which endears him to his contemporaries – the carpenters, builders and plumbers who went to school with him and still live and work close by. Beatriz, with her thick dark curls, does day duty, rustling up some mean tortillas for her hungry customers before Lorenzo returns to take on the night-time bar crowd. Evening drinking kicks off on the pavement tables but if there's an important football match, particularly a game between Madrid and Barcelona, the room inside bursts.

This bar is also big into lottery tickets which are a national obsession. Ever since Spain launched its first lottery back in 1763 the payouts have escalated. Now, the richest, '*El Gordo*' – the fat one – is drawn out of huge golden drums on TV in December and as tickets are limited you can imagine the excitement. I'm well into it already.

Lorenzo and Beatriz's bar hasn't been altered in years. A family, whose grainy photos from a century past hang round the walls of its single room, has been content to leave well alone. The bar inside is edged with art deco pink and green ceramics, there are encaustic tiles on the floor in grey and cream, marble-topped tables and the cleanest lavatory in Mallorca.

Although there are only a dozen houses separating Sancho's bar from Lorenzo's both families in this small village work in happy tandem. When one takes a day off, the other stays open. Both serve the best coffee in the world, but as Sancho's bar is the nearest, I guess this is where I'll regularly make footfall.

———

A fortnight later and the house now sorted, I'm reciting the drill for survival to my friends' children, George who is eight and his four-year-old sister Rosie, hoping to make it sound an adventure. George is quiet and listens intently. Rosie, distracted, is unhappy to discover there is no TV but for some reason perks up at the prospect of sleeping under a mosquito net. My nervousness at how they'll manage begins to abate by suppertime. I've cobbled together a charcoal grill outside and, with the children happily enjoying a meal of chicken and salad made from the wild spinach, fennel and herbs they've picked earlier in the field, everyone begins to relax. As a full moon floats up into the warm summer sky and stars begin to glitter, a strange squeaking creeps into our conversation.

'Mummy, what's that in the tree?' asks George who is sitting opposite me, staring into an expanse of wild olive trees in the field. His mother gets up to peer into the semi-darkness. 'Something's running up the tree,' he insists. She concentrates on the tree but can't make out a thing, telling him, finally, to be quiet.

A little while later I catch George, his eyes wide, still looking in the direction of the olive trees. He has stopped eating and is riveted. I move to join him and follow his gaze. 'Why are there rats in the trees?' he wants to know.

It is, indeed, quite a sight. Dozens of rat-like creatures big and small are hurtling along the branches like squirrels, squealing and calling to one another. George doesn't offer up any more observations, so I quickly suggest the children get ready for bed while the rest of us spend what's left of the evening trying not to make mention of unwelcome rodents.

I have to fly out to Britain late that night, leaving my friends to handle the vermin problem as best they can. Three days later I'm back to tales of wonder and woe. George has spent most of the time in his bedroom, windows firmly closed on the hottest night of the year, afraid the creatures might creep into the house. They have all, I am grandly informed, been kept awake anyway by the sound of them jumping up and down on the roof although, luckily, they have not seen any sign during the day. 'Rats take siestas,' Rosie pronounces as she fetches her bucket and spade to retreat to the beach. I am a heartbeat away from following her.

I clap eyes close up on one of the culprits the day Rosie and George depart. Quietly reading in a chair under the vine I feel something watching. There, framed in a smoke outlet in the bread oven, are two bright eyes and two furry little ears.

Its face is very cute, less rodent-like, more bushbaby, but when I look again it turns and, with a twitch of a rat-like tail, disappears. I put the book down and go to investigate but there isn't a trace. Well, that isn't quite true. At the back of the oven, a pile of almond husks has been neatly stacked, each husk has a hole where the essence of the almond has clearly been sucked out. It occurs to me that I obviously live in a house with many more inhabitants than I'd bargained for. I'm just not sure what, exactly, lurks within its deepest recesses.

Thankfully the 'squirrels', as I have now less menacingly dubbed these nocturnal athletes, have decided to lower their profile on my return to the island, cavorting on my roof a little less regularly. Or perhaps I'm just getting used to their partying, falling asleep regardless. Even the offer of a life-changing new TV job with CBS, which has come sooner than I expected and got me thinking, is not enough to keep me awake at night. Something about this place must be working.

Certainly the ants are. There must be millions of them in Mallorca, burrowing and building in the hot sun. I am absorbed with their cleverness and often drop crumbs to see how many race in to lift seemingly impossible weights over huge obstacles, like my big toe, hauling their booty back to their nests in the ground. Only the cicadas in the trees have the same busy energy as the ants in the hottest part of the day. The big black ants with the sharp bite mainly live in massive mounds in the field but come to the house to fight for every morsel with their tinier cousins who have made themselves at home under all the floors and in cracks in every corner. Ants pile out when the fridge opens, clean up the work surface in the kitchen and march in straight black lines up the whitewashed walls in the sitting room. If I am not careful they can also sneak in under the lid of the sugar bowl or burrow away in the tea caddy. I have also known them chew through plastic lids to get at rice or spaghetti. With ants I am always on patrol.

It was because ants had wriggled into my tea leaves and spoiled my morning cuppa that I set off earlier than normal to the village to buy a fresh supply. Walking back and in no particular hurry I stop near a ramshackle collection of huts, a smallholding, shielded from the road by canes lashed together to act as a kind of screen. I must have passed it dozens of times, not taking much notice except to register there were a few orange and lemon trees in a scrubby-looking field with hens, ducks and goats hobbled, bound from one ankle to the other, to prevent their escape. I have never seen anyone in the building but today I notice the place is well fortified. A tall metal gate is shuttered with a big padlock and through a chink in the canes I can make out, almost within touching distance, a female dog anchored to a kennel by a short, heavy chain. She hasn't made a sound. The kennel I notice faces west and has little shade. The young mongrel, lying on a concrete slab, is dejected.

I don't know quite what to do or who to speak to. The dog is lying down, but as I look more closely I can see there is a bowl of water close by, she seems to be in quite good shape and is certainly not starving. I try to hope that this, then, is just a temporary measure and that whoever owns her will be here soon to let her off the chain so that she can run around.

My shoulders are starting to burn and as I move to look for something in my bag which might protect them an old man on an elderly motor scooter suddenly appears. He's wearing a flat cap, is about five foot high and doesn't look happy to see me, although I try to be pleasant. '*Buenos días*,' I venture with my best smile. He just lifts his head, a backwards nod, in acknowledgement. And that is it. He goes to park his bike round the corner and returns, with a limp, to unlock the gate.

I wish I could speak Mallorquín so that I can ask about this dog but I am not sure where it will lead and the man is obviously in no mood to help me. So I turn away, trying to think of who to ask, who might know about him.

Unable to shake the image of the dog from my mind, I decide to invite my nearest neighbours to dinner to quiz them. Emmy Lou lives in a finca on the hill higher up the valley which she found twenty-five years ago. An old man occupied the house then, one of the few Mallorquíns who stayed to try and keep the old place from falling into ruin but Emmy Lou and her family were prepared to give it a new lease of life so they settled in when the old man moved out. Emmy Lou, like so many hippies in this part of Mallorca, washed up on the shores of the Balearics back in the sixties on a wave of free love and flower power. Initial landfall for them was Ibiza but with growing broods and little money most seemed to find their way to Mallorca, settling a little inland in farmsteads with no running water and no power but promising the good life.

When I was first introduced to her, Emmy Lou sent me poetry in praise of the beauty of the place. One, I remember, was called 'An Ode to the Vale of Tranquillity'. It was a bit off the mark especially when Emmy Lou's dog went AWOL. 'John-O!' she'd yell at the top of her voice, shattering my siesta. Emmy Lou has many good points, but trying to discuss, for example, the state of the road or the water supply is like trying to wrestle with bubblegum. Her ability to talk a subject out and decide nothing is exasperating. I was in the TV business where interviewing people meant sound-bite responses of three minutes max. An entire life story could be told in three minutes. It was more than I gave my dearest friends. Emmy Lou would take some getting used to and she, me.

My other neighbours are of the same vintage as Emmy Lou, artists of one kind or another or musicians who in the early days helped one another repair their respective ruins. Like all close-knit support groups they also get a certain combustion out of the many simmering feuds that regularly bubble up. I soon discovered that becoming involved in their *cirque du soleil* is a bit risky for a newcomer like me – friendships stretching back many decades take some figuring. Emmy Lou, for example, has a strained relationship with Lauren, a fellow American, who lives nearby. They are pretty much the same age and ditched the fathers of their respective children at about the same time, leaving them both to battle on in straitened circumstances. You would have thought that they would be sympathetic to one another, but no. Perhaps it's because they share the same stretch of pot-holed road, maybe it's because they have seen too much of one another and their comings and goings over too many years.

Lauren is slightly built and blonde, in her mid-forties, with a talent for reiki and other holistic treatments that she ministers to grateful customers who suffer especially from bad backs. She travels in a beat-up jeep all over the island and knows people as only those who ease pain can. Lauren lives on her own in an old house in need of repair and yet with drive and determination continues to colour her life with adventure. To raise cash for her travels Lauren rents out her finca for months at a time, as does Emmy Lou. Emmy Lou has a *casita*, a small one-roomed house that she lets usually to young men looking for work in the building trade. Up until now we three have kept a friendly distance, but as usual in a small place where there's information to trade, such an amicable arrangement doesn't last long. When I phone to arrange a time to meet, both Lauren and Emmy Lou are willing. They want to discuss the state of the road; I'm keener to know about the dog.

There's the most heavenly scent cascading off the honeysuckle mounded at the side of the house when Lauren arrives first, looking pained. Emmy Lou turns up soon after with

Carter, her blond son with his firm jaw, probably in his twenties, in tow. Lauren will have watched Carter as a child growing up in the valley, but you wouldn't know it judging by her manner. It's hard to pin down, just dismissive I suppose and Carter, in turn, is lukewarm towards her. I make to pour some very large glasses of best Binissalem red, leaving the three of them to circle the encampment.

When I return the conversation's getting heated as they warm to the grievances both share over the road. The discussion starts okay, each agreeing that soon it will be almost impossible for vehicles to get up or down as summer storms have washed away what little surface it has. Just when I begin to think we're in for a convivial night, out of nowhere, Emmy Lou launches a sidewinder at Lauren, accusing her renters of wrecking the road by driving along it at great speeds. Lauren flings something back to the effect that Emmy Lou shouldn't even be using the road. I forget the exact reasons why. 'What are we going to do about fixing it?' My voice strains to drown the vibes.

Lauren calms down a bit and then says, 'Tarmac is the only solution, end-to-end tarmac.'

But Emmy Lou, blazing, is having none of it. 'The last thing I want is a super-highway. Why can't we repair it by digging out channels and back-filling with stone?'

'Oh, yes. And are *you* going to get out the shovel, Emmy Lou?' Lauren prods, as sweet as apple pie.

'How much can each of us pay to repair the road?' I try

another tack knowing that it is all pretty futile by now. It is plain neither of them is prepared to spend a cent on the road as long as the other is using it. Lauren says she has no money and will have to take out a loan but she will only do so, anyway, if the road gets tarmacked. Emmy Lou has no cash either and if she had she wouldn't waste it on something toxic like tar.

A nighthawk shrieks as it hunts in the field outside but as no one is showing any sign of going home, I decide to change the subject. 'Where can I find the best spring water in the district?' I brightly lob into the gloom.

Now this is something Emmy Lou obviously feels qualified to pronounce upon having been here for years. She has no hesitation in declaring that the Font des Bosc, a spring about two miles away, is the finest but Lauren has different ideas and is not about to let an opportunity to outsmart Emmy Lou slip by. She makes an announcement that she has had Font des Bosc water analysed only recently and the report has come back: 'Thirty per cent sheep shit, forty per cent rat shit and thirty per cent unspecified shit.'

This juicy bit of information hangs over the four of us for all of a second. Then Carter, having kept schtum until now, says, 'But Lauren, I have been drinking that water all my life.'

Lauren doesn't miss a beat. 'And why does that not surprise me, Carter?'

Carter, not getting the joke and out-classed, shuts up but his mother is not for letting this joust end yet. She and Lauren chew on until I bring up the subject of the dog. Did they know it was tied to a short chain so it can hardly move? Emmy Lou says, unfortunately, that's the way it is here, but dogs are better treated now than they were when she first arrived. I then get a lecture on the way things used to be. Large sheep-dogs were dragged behind horse-drawn carts, attempting and sometimes failing to keep up at the end of a rope.

Carter jumps in. 'You can't come here and tell local people how to live their lives,' he snarls at me. 'The dog has always been chained. It is fed and watered and that's the way it is.'

I try one last shot. 'But can't you speak to the man who owns her?'

'Can't you offer to take the dog for a walk? You must pass it several times a day.'

As if. I now desperately want the night to end but just as I begin to think they might finally say their goodbyes, one of Emmy Lou's cats with all its kittens arrives.

Apparently Emmy Lou has started bringing left-over food from the village restaurant where she's head cook up to her house in the valley. There she dispenses her largesse to her cat, Tiddles. But news of free food has spread all over the district and now Emmy Lou is inundated with starving cats desperate for grub. What's worse, hungry mother cats bring their little ones too, so that now there is an army of vociferous kittens in the valley. I had wondered why, eating out under the stars, I was accosted by lots of appealing faces, never real-ising that the kittens were feral. I gave them what I could, thinking they were just a breed of opportunistic cats who really had proper homes with owners who loved and cared for them. Who wouldn't?

By the light of a lantern, these kittens would jump up the stone steps, scramble over the flagstones to my front door, their little tails trembling to stop themselves tumbling. Often mothers would push the kittens forward to let them eat first, not taking a thing for themselves. Coming so soon after the dog on his chain this was the last thing I wanted to know, another harsh lesson, the abandoned cats of Mallorca.

The sight of kittens is too much for Lauren. Her own pet cat has been badly mauled, she says, 'And all thanks to you, Emmy Lou. You are personally responsible for all the cat fights because you feed all these strays.'

Having delivered her parting shot, Lauren heads home, the cat and her kittens choosing to trot off after Emmy Lou into the night as I make a mental note to always carry cat food with me and never to invite these two adversaries to the same gig again.

Next morning I am in the mood to tackle the towering bougainvillea, which has thrown itself exuberantly over the road. It is in full purple but has taken to catching and tearing with its thorns anyone who walks by. Grabbing my secateurs and gloves off the kitchen table I launch into the shrub, the problem of what to do about the dog on the chain bugging me. I guess I must have been occupied for about an hour when 'Buenos días, Señora,' floats over and there through the bougainvillea is an elderly couple wearing sun bonnets, complimenting me on how *bonita* – how beautiful – my garden is. They are telling me they're on their way to visit their old home further up the road. It is so very hot and, although they are both well protected with their straw hats, I ask them if they'd like a glass of water. They say they would, and they come and sit with me under the shade of the vine for a while.

I learn that they regularly walk up the hill from the village to the ruin behind my house, which, many years ago, was once their home. The roof fell in only recently, they say, now it's a pile of rubble but it still holds enough memories for them to sit amidst it, thinking of the past and enjoying the fact that they still own the old place and the land all around. In spring they collect armfuls of blue iris in what used to be their garden or gather tender tips of wild asparagus from the roadside. There is always something for them to do. The old man must be in his eighties and has a sweet face, the skin around his deep-set brown eyes crinkled with the sun. Funnily enough, his wife looks almost identical, they could be brother and sister: the same height, the same colouring and the same way of speaking.

After a time I ask them about the man who owns the dog and am told that he has met with tragedy in his life. His oldest son, Nico, was almost killed in a motorcycle accident when he was on his way home one night after finishing work at a restaurant. The accident left him paralysed on one side so he can now no longer use his arm and leg and it is feared he has brain damage. Nico was hospitalised in Son Dureta on the outskirts of Palma for months. The old man pauses and shakes his head. While this boy was close to death his mother died of cancer. The family has been shattered. The dog, called Kendi, belongs to Nico but now no one walks her and she is tied up. There is nothing anyone can do, the old man shrugs, this is the way of people here, they have dogs to protect their property and most of them are on short chains. He tries to reassure me, saying that the dog will be let off her chain during the day and be given exercise, but I am not convinced.

His wife finishes her glass of water and prompts her husband to leave so that they can get back to the village before noon and I try to put Kendi to the back of my mind without success, the beauty of the day darkened by the plight of a dog.

two

The BBC is under pressure to find me work. A press conference, heralding the new autumn schedule, is hijacked by the tabloids demanding to know where I am, what I'm doing and whether I'm still being paid. And while we're at it, how much exactly am I getting? My gardening leave from *Breakfast* that summer is clearly not going to wiggle away unnoticed. So in the meantime, asks the director-general, will I agree to front a new weekly fashion programme, *The Clothes Show*, while the BBC considers my long-term future and short term gets the press off its back? I'm not mightily impressed at being parachuted into a show whose producer has already picked his presenter, in this case, the fashion designer Jeff Banks, but the DG is insistent. So I dump my sandals and shorts and fly off to Birmingham to meet Jeff and the team.

The BBC announces my new role and I lob in my own bit

of information: I have also been hired to co-anchor CBS's new coast-to-coast current affairs show, *West 57th*, a younger version of the iconic *60 Minutes* programme from the same network, which will mean me commuting back and forth to the States. As both shows are due to start later in the year I have a month or two to figure out how I can manage the workload and also take care of business in Mallorca.

It hasn't taken long for me to discover that candles aren't romantic after all. Reading in bed is downright dangerous under a flimsy mosquito net. The roof tiles absorb the sun's daytime intensity and turn my bedroom into an oven at night. With rats dancing on the tiles and mosquitoes buzzing inside the net what I need, urgently, is a new roof, electricity and, oh yes, mosquito blinds at all the windows. More vital than anything, I have to fix the water supply. All this in the few short months before work begins on two continents.

———

Waking to a crystal-clear morning in the middle of September is delicious. I feel I can tackle anything. Like cleaning out the cupboard under the sink where I know a cockroach lurks and turning the mattresses before going in search of the water I ordered by tanker, a week back. I decide to wrestle with the beds first and am upstairs struggling with a heavy mattress when suddenly a fiery little scorpion jumps out and races across the floor, its tail waggling up and down, very, very angry at being disturbed. Its mate leaps out to join it, quickly followed by their babies. And all from under my pillow. To think I am sleeping with this lot.

The whole caboodle disappear down a crack in the floor – every last man of them – and I steel myself to resolutely refuse to think of the damage they are capable of inflicting. I suppose I am becoming a bit inured to creepy-crawlies although a scorpion in the bed takes a bit of beating. I give the mattress turning a miss and head to the village for a coffee because I need a slug of something strong to set me off on the trail of the elusive water cart.

The flock of long-legged sheep that graze the rough ground around the village are walking up the track towards me with their shepherd, Jesus. Jesus is in his early sixties and has a thatch of greying hair. He's taking his sheep to the land he owns on the hillside, fenced off with bits of old wire and tin, where they lodge during the day, sheltering from the sun under holm oaks while he goes to his own home to sleep. Jesus's gangly Mallorquín sheepdog trudges alongside him on a lead of old rope, his black coat covered in fine dust. Both are exhausted after a night spent watching the flock. As I pass them on the road, Jesus tips his head and gives a fleeting smile.

Sancho's son Paco bounces into the bar as I arrive. He is a tall boy with an open face, an engaging manner and feet that float outwards as he walks. His mother, Pepita, obviously loves him to bits. Paco works part-time for an American couple who own a boat and has started augmenting his native Spanish with what he believes are über-cool expressions.

'How are you, Paco?' I ask. And out pops, 'Feeling no pain, Sal.'

Half an hour later, the bloke behind the front desk of the water office in nearby Andratx is putting me through agony. He is insisting I cannot have any water as the road to my house is so bad. Water tankers criss-cross the island daily, filled with spring water – *agua potable* – delivering up to forty tons wherever needed. I want a ten-ton load and there is only one firm in the district with a tanker small enough to negotiate my track. This is it, in the market town of Andratx, three miles away.

I try not to panic as this fellow who holds my future in his hands goes on to say that one of his tanker drivers is in hospital with serious injuries after tipping and falling down an incline on a road not nearly as rough as mine. I suppose I can't blame him, as the track is like a river bed with great boulders and lumps erupting along its length. I don't think there is a single smooth spot, and a tanker, with its huge weight, is going to really rock and roll. Just as I am about to sit down and weep, he tells me to telephone Santiago.

I want to leap out and hug Santiago Monserrat when he arrives on his bright red tractor later that day with a small six-ton water bowser behind him. Santiago is wearing a baseball hat set slightly back off his cheery face and with one hand on his hip, the other on the steering wheel, to this girl he is like a gift from the gods. Still or fizzy, he shouts over the fence as he begins pumping spring water into my *deposito*.

'Will you come next week?'

'*Sí, sí, no problemas,*' he says as he pockets 2,000 pesetas and chugs off down the hill.

I wonder if Emmy Lou and Lauren might come to an agreement about doing up the road now that we three are totally dependent on Santiago. 'If the road was in better condition,' I implore over the phone, 'the large water tanker would make the journey. Surely this is vital for us all?'

Neither, however, is remotely interested in discussing water or the state of the road again. They have no money and that is the end of that.

Desperate days call for desperate measures so I phone up Gunther. Francine answers and goes to get him.

'Gunther,' I begin, 'can you tell me who you got to drill for water?'

'No, I don't remember.' Gunther still isn't feeling neighbourly. 'Why do you want to know?'

'I'm thinking of drilling in my field. Is there plenty in your well?'

'No. Water is in short supply and in any case it is contaminated.'

'Contaminated with what?'

'With arsenic.'

'Arsenic?'

'Yup, and it is the colour of shit. Brown.'

I try not to take this personally but it's obvious I can't rely on Gunther. I'm not sure of my next move. Drilling for water seems to be the only sensible option when everyone is at odds over how to care for the road. So if I am going to drill, I begin to reason, I'll have to find water first. I'm going to need a water diviner.

A bit of detective work later and I am in a restaurant in Andratx, which has a fountain spouting spring water in its courtyard. Not surprising then that the owner, a lugubrious little man, does a bit of dowsing on the side and agrees to come over to my place the next day. I just wish he looked happier about it. Nevertheless he turns up on time, kitted out in black wearing what I take are his best black leather loafers, a yellow duster-like cloth with two twigs under his arm. He manages a strangled '*buenos*' to me and sets off through the long grass, twigs not yet twitching. I pad behind him, neither of us saying a word. He knows what he is looking for and I am completely absorbed in the quest.

When he gets to a fig tree by the boundary of the field, suddenly the twigs, like poltergeists, get active. He moves in a small circle, round and round, his arms like metronomes. 'You have lots of water here,' he says, then quietly, '*mucho, mucho*' as the twigs swing back and forth with great and remarkable energy.

Soon I am deep in negotiation with a one-legged Swede who my dowser says is the expert hereabouts on the business of drilling for water. Erland is in his sixties and lost his leg putting a new roof on Emmy Lou's house ten years back, but that is another story. He has branched out into delving for water and is telling me he will oversee the enormous drilling machine while I am away working. We get the financial side sorted straight off. It will cost the equivalent of five thousand pounds just to get the machine to the field. Then each metre drilled and each metre lined with pipe has a price. Plus, if I strike lucky, there will be a pump to buy. More importantly I have to decide if I am going to drill where the dowser's twigs twitched and, if so, am I absolutely certain I want to gamble on them because finding water underground is notoriously difficult in Mallorca? I could lose the lot. Another long drag on his cigarette and Erland's sorrowful blue eyes fix on me. I get the feeling he is itching me to throw the dice.

'I don't have much time to waste,' I venture, thinking of my earlier encounter with the water haulier in Andratx and my travel plans later that year. 'I have come this far, let's have a go.'

Erland eases himself on to his good leg and with surprising agility, hops off to close the deal with the drillers in Palma.

I've had enough excitement for one day, so quickly, before anyone or anything else turns up, I grab the old key from its hook and lock the heavy front door. Secreting the key under a rock, I'm off for a walk. The earth is still parched, dust dances round my feet as I stride out through fields of almond and olive, up through the woods of sweet pine and holm oak to the track that will take me to the coast. The air is different here, with a movement and freshness that makes today's trek a joy.

These footpaths will have been used for centuries by local people moving animals to graze on the mountains in the summer months, or to reach hill settlements further up the island. There are small huts, *casitas*, dotted around the slopes, their roofs broken but the stone walls still intact, now offering shelter for wild goats. Grey and white, brown and black, some with massive corkscrew horns, it seems there are goats claiming the heights round every crag. These inquisitive creatures who live off wild lavender and cistus know where spring water pours out of the rock and are very taken with strangers on their patch. I am told they are indigenous to Mallorca. They make me laugh with their sudden bursts of feigned surprise and flight.

Without warning, the wide track turns tiny into a narrower path which splits off in another direction. You have to know – and remember – which one leads to where you want to go. There is no sign of the sea here, all around is a mountain-scape of dry scrub. I have been here before and know to take the path downhill towards a dry river bed, jumping from stone to stone to make progress, before climbing up the steep incline to reach the top of another hill and its sudden, spectacular view. Cliffs, hundreds of feet high, veer into the distance, on and on, almost to infinity, the blue Mediterranean crashing against the rocks as seabirds cruise-control the currents. It is a kind of primeval vista which must have caught and held the moment for so many people, millennia before.

The track to the left eases me along the cliff top towards

the old monastery of Sa Trapa another hour away. An order of Trappist monks came here hundreds of years ago, loved the setting, and began irrigating and building a hermetic life overlooking the unspoiled island of Dragonera. Perched precipitously on the headland edge, the community dwindled at the beginning of the twentieth century until only a couple of old monks were left, hanging on until Sa Trapa fell into total ruin. Today it is a designated protected site and work has begun on its preservation. As it will add another hour to my walk if I step off the path and go down to Sa Trapa I decide to carry on, climbing higher to the mountain pass which tips me into a steep descent, down to the fishing village of San Telm below.

After my long walk, I'm feeling a little less frantic about life back at the hacienda. Although I can't believe I'm now engaged in drilling for something as basic as water so soon after buying the place, I have a horrible feeling hand-to-hand combat over electricity looms. The island gives the impression it's up to speed. Heavy electric cables swing uglily yet practically along all the streets and water comes out of taps like other European countries, but local politicians make such heavy weather of everything I'm beginning to wonder if, as an incomer, I'm equipped for the challenge. When the sun shines from the heavens on a day like this, though, it's hard not to convince myself, I am.

Eight hundred years ago something that appeals to the bruiser in me happened here in San Telm. It was a similar sunny day when the great fleet of a hundred and fifty sailing ships of the Christian king Jaime I dropped anchor to face five thousand Muslims lined up on the shore. Jaime was just twenty-one years old, apparently a hunk, well over six feet tall with red hair and blue eyes, who had come determined to reconquer Mallorca and remove the Moors after three hundred years of Islam. Fifteen hundred Arabs were crushed along the coast that September day, changing the destiny of the island and San Telm. Soon after a protective castle went up which still guards the bay today.

San Telm is one of the few villages on the coast in Mallorca that Jaime would still recognise if he stepped ashore now. The tiny island of Panteleu, 250 yards from the beach, in Jaime's words, 'a long crossbow shot from the mainland', remains unspoiled, a colony of shearwater sea birds mumbling and grumbling on it as night falls. I wish Jaime were around now. He could prove jolly useful.

Lungfuls of mountain air and mighty fights have made me hungry and luckily there are plenty of cafés in San Telm from which to choose. So many restaurants on the island serve up hearty, heavy fare which palls very quickly. There is only so much calamari grille or paella a girl can handle. And the salads, which are universally uninspiring, arrive on a big platter covered in what looks like half a cabbage with man-size tomato slices and a tin of tuna dumped on top. Proper Mallorquín cooking is a rare find.

In San Telm there are several restaurants that venture into

tempting territory. The fish served at the oceanside restaurant at Cala Conills is one. It looks out on to Dragonera into the setting sun, a romantic venue reached by a sea-washed path up from the shore. Another is the family-run restaurant of Chez Janneau on the opposite side of the bay, which carves jamón serrano, ham from the black pig on the mainland, and other Spanish delicacies to locals dining under pine trees. The restaurants huddled together on the pier are also spectacularly sited, and with their home cooking and special cakes ordered fresh from a small bakery in Andratx, no wonder there is a constant coming and going throughout the day.

Most of the cafés and bars along the bay are owned by families from my village who come each summer to make a living from the tourists. It is a source of wonderment to me how they have resisted the temptation to develop and wreck while all around others cave in and concrete over the beauty of the coast. I would love to have been here in the 1950s when the only road in to the resort was a dirt track through the hills and a few shacks and fishing huts lined the shore, but today, nevertheless, San Telm is charming with an end-of-season air as holidaymakers begin to plot their journey home.

Normally I'd pop into Janneau's café for a cold beer and sandwich but it's his day off so instead I make for the café overlooking the bay further down the road where three middle-aged sisters from the village serve home-made food through the year. The café caters mainly for workmen and locals because its prices are reasonable. The oldest of the sisters, Caty, is leaning on a chair under the blue-and-white awning when I breeze in looking for a bite to eat. Caty's speciality is arroz marinera, a rice dish eaten like a soup flavoured with a rich sea stock and cooked in the traditional way with mussels and cod and squid. For a few pesetas you can get this along with a flan (a crème caramel) and coffee. It is a dish to share so instead, I opt for a pa amb oli to go with my beer, a real filler: two large slices of wholemeal bread rubbed with ripe tomatoes, olive oil and layers of jamón serrano.

Caty has a cheeky diffidence towards her regulars. She glides with a kind of theatrical absentmindedness, swiping her tables with a damp cloth as she gestures customers to their seats. An elderly American professor is having his usual fish of the day with his friend, a German artist from the village. They've taken the best seats in the corner under the canopy. 'Caty, you're looking particularly fetching,' one of them shouts across to her, 'what have you got for our lunch?'

These two come each weekday to tease Caty and take the sea air and with their shiny tonsures could easily be mistaken for the last couple of monks to make it out of Sa Trapa. The American professor is, incongruously, sporting a thick padded vest on this very warm day. He obviously feels the cold. Caty treats them to a giggle and a dismissive wave of her cloth before calling their order to her younger sister slaving in the kitchen.

The pair of them are here for the afternoon. I, however,

have tons to do and although the beer is proving a bit of a break, twenty minutes later I'm off, back to the village, mindful of taking a shortcut round the hill by the cemetery so that I won't have to pass Kendi listening for me in her kennel on the way up to my house.

———

It has poured down overnight. Great crashes of thunder roll over the village followed by lightning, vicious and unrelenting. The dogs in the fincas higher up the valley fall silent as an unexpected rush of wind whips through the pine trees, pushing and bending the cypresses before suddenly dropping as the rain begins its drenching again. Storms in Mallorca often start with the slightest of changes, a few pale clouds in a clear blue sky, or a thin, warming breeze on a still day. Soon the deluge will begin, smashing into the red, parched land, which, overwhelmed, spills it straight into the nearest *torrente* along with what's left of my track to the village.

After the battering, it's a joy to unlock the shutters and step outside, to smell the hot earth after its cooling. Sodden tendrils of vine litter the ground along with dozens of scarlet baby flowers blown from the pomegranate tree, but this morning I have no time to stand and stare. I have had a phone call from CBS who need me to fly to Kenya to check unsubstantiated rumours that elephants are being slaughtered for their ivory in a country which depends for its livelihood on safari tourism. It will be an international scandal if we can uncover evidence, so somehow I need to manage to manoeuvre myself down the washed-away track that morning to get to the airport and London, where I'm booked on an overnight flight for Nairobi.

Erland now knows he's in charge of water drilling while I'm away. The rig has been booked for this coming week and we cannot cancel. 'I can handle it,' he assures me, 'have a good trip and keep fingers crossed', as the car and I go free fall, slithering through the mud, lurching in and out of the newly exposed potholes, to somehow reach the bottom of the hill before the car stalls – right outside Kendi's kennel. In that small moment, in the time it takes to turn the key and re-start the engine, I have glimpsed what I feared: a creature in utter misery. Wet to the bone, still anchored by a short chain to the cold damp concrete, she is looking up at me as if to ask 'what have I done to deserve this?' What's worse, I know more torrential rain is forecast for her later in the day. And because I know there is nothing I can do, just then, to release her from this hell, I'm afraid I begin to cry as I pull away.

At the airport, thousands of holidaymakers are arriving from all over Europe. Private jets ferry owners of luxury yachts to sail from up-market marinas round the coast. Mercs and Audis queue for parking space. This is becoming one of the wealthiest islands in the world but not a single peseta leaves the government purse to help care for its hundreds of abandoned and cruelly treated cats and dogs. There is no animal rescue organisation that has the power to come and release

Kendi in my absence. As I board the plane for London, I begin to realise that it will be down to me to deal with her release on my return.

The film made in Kenya over the next ten days leads to a dramatic change in the international CITES law on poaching as footage of elephants, mothers and babies, hacked to death for whatever minuscule amount of ivory they possess, sickens America. In the northern hills of Kora, the *Born Free* conservationist, George Adamson, old and sinewy, but passionate still, finally found us the evidence we were seeking. Through the bush near his camp, he took us, on foot, to a clearing where the noise of thousands of flies round the headless, swollen carcasses of a small family herd soundtracked, prime time, across the States a couple of weeks later.

George Adamson lived long enough to witness the world's revulsion that brought about a ban on the ivory trade but confronting poachers early one morning after hearing shots outside his camp, George Adamson was murdered.

———

It is a grim weekday afternoon. I'm in my office in New York, under pressure to get the film cut and ready for airing on *West 57th* that Saturday night, when Erland phones. The weather has been so bad on the island, he tells me, that the drilling rig couldn't get up the road, but the men have now arrived, he declares, and are ready to begin. I had quite forgotten the drilling in my rush to get the hard-fought-for footage back to the States and here is Erland urgently needing to know if I want a rig to start on my land first.

Did I hear him right? 'Where else would a rig be drilling first if not with me?'

'Well,' Erland hesitated, 'Emmy Lou's.'

'*What*? Emmy Lou is drilling? I thought she had no money?'

'Well, I don't know about that,' Erland diplomatically stalls for time, 'but Emmy Lou found out you were going to drill so she's going to have a go too. So is Lauren. They've had their own diviners up here. They're both drilling for water.'

'*Both* drilling?'

This means three of us are using money to find water which we may or may not discover when we could have clubbed together and had tankerloads of fresh spring water delivered for evermore if we had done up the road instead.

Out of frustration I tell Erland to get the driller to start on Emmy Lou's land first. If she can't find water, I threaten, then I won't bother going ahead. It will serve her right if there isn't any. Erland says he'll report back.

When Erland eventually phones again he's in a bit of a state. 'The good news,' he starts off, 'is the driller tackled Emmy Lou's and Lauren's land first, although they're mad at you, and at fifty metres they found lots of water...' he pauses. 'But I'm afraid we've gone down a great depth on your land and there's no water.'

'No water? But there must be water. Emmy Lou and Lauren have found it, haven't they?'

An image of we three women like the witches in *Macbeth*, hubbling and troubling, flickers across my mind.

'What do you want me to do now?' asks Erland.

'What on earth do you suggest?' I counter.

To my astonishment, Erland glibly announces, 'The drilling machine can go down a few more metres, it will be a risk, mind, it doesn't normally go that deep, but do you want me to do it? It will cost more.' Erland is obviously ratcheting up the drama and enjoying every ounce of this affair; I suppose I can't blame him.

'Yes, of course,' I finally demur.

When the phone rings half an hour later, he can hardly speak. 'We've got it. Tons and tons of water, from deep down. It was so touch and go, I can't believe it, but we've struck a great seam.'

'Well, thank God for that,' is all I am able to muster.

The next few weeks are frenzied, first, filming for *The Clothes Show*, a surprise success in the UK, then on to Switzerland for *West 57th* on the track of a US fugitive – *West 57th*, by the way, would also like an update on the Loch Ness Monster and Jack the Ripper as well as a profile of the Russian chess champion Garry Kasparov in Bilbao and another with Prince Charles at Sandringham. When I eventually manage to get to Mallorca in late January, aware that my relationship with my neighbours is now a bit dodgy, I'm ready for a rest.

The island couldn't be more inviting, dressed as if for a wedding, with pink and white blossom adorning every almond tree and because there isn't a breath of wind, there it will shimmer, like confetti, for almost a month. This is *La Calma d'Enero*, the calm of January, the lull at the beginning of the year when blue skies and short, sunny days bring everyone out into the fields to make bonfires and be busy. It was this gentle weather that enticed Chopin over a hundred years ago to a cold monastery in Valldemossa further up the island where, in spite of angry locals who didn't like him and the onset of rain which nearly killed him, he managed to compose some of his loveliest preludes. Some things never change.

I'm dreading Kendi and what I'll find after all these weeks away and even wonder whether she'll still be there, but as I round the corner into the road leading towards my house I can't believe it, the old man is talking animatedly to someone and he has Kendi with him, on a lead. Her ears are pricked and she looks happy to be included in whatever they are discussing. I would love to stop and say hello to her, but the old man, as usual, doesn't look inviting so I ease past and suddenly I feel much, much better.

The looming problem of truculent neighbours lifts at the thought that maybe this could be the start of something good for poor Kendi if her owner has started taking her for walks. Maybe I can ask if I can take her into the hills one day as well, so that we can explore and find new walks together. My delight at the sight of Kendi off her chain doesn't diminish even when I discover that while I've been away the walls and furniture of the old house have been covered in a white, powdery mould from damp.

Opening the creaking shutters to let in freshness will help and anyway, my first job before I shake off the television cobwebs is to inspect my new water supply which I notice has had its own little house built at the edge of the field. Erland has been working hard. He's already had the water tested and I gather I owe Gunther an apology because, although drinkable, once the water is exposed to air it does indeed turn shit-brown. There's iron in the water which has to settle before it turns crystal clear which means another *deposito* will have to be dug close by. Compared to this, I'm beginning to think Santiago with his water bowser is a luxury I won't be able to do without. Nothing on the island is ever straightforward.

———

There's a big blue-black bee sucking the juice out of the jasmine, its weight flattening the petals. I have never seen a bee like it, glistening and buzzing around the garden in the morning sun. I am so taken up with this huge bug that I hardly notice the man inspecting my house.

Erland is with him and he's smiling. 'Meet my good friend Boris,' he says. 'You asked for a builder, well, Boris is the one who is going to help you restore your house now you've got plenty of water.' And like a cat that's proudly nabbed a big fat mouse, Erland thrusts Boris at me and slopes off.

Boris is German and a bit fey so it takes a little while before he gathers enough momentum to tell me what he'd like to do with the house. It doesn't help that I'm suspicious.

His hands don't look like a builder's hands, his fingers, constantly fidgeting with a strand of long silvery hair that keeps flopping over his eyes, are tapered and manicured. He doesn't have the physique of a builder either. Boris is delicate and is kitted out in a vibrant orange smock over pale blue trousers and yellow espadrilles. I'd lay any amount of money that I'm looking at another artist. Turns out he is and, as I will discover, a good one too, but to earn a living he has to build and is keen to get his talented hands on my place, the sooner the better.

I try dampening his enthusiasm, there is no electricity, but it doesn't put him off. He can handle the generator left by Johnny, he says assertively, prising open the dunny where the clapped-out machine resides, and now that I have water, he enthuses, we can pump enough to mix cement. He wants to bring out the beauty of the old finca, to give me special places outside where I can sit and relax surrounded by nature.

'What I want to know,' I interject, before he gets too carried away, 'is can you make it vermin proof?'

'Vat do you mean?' he demands in a thick German accent.

'Rats jump about on my roof,' I say, 'and any moment I fear they'll be in the house co-habiting with me. How can you stop them?'

Boris then launches off into a rhapsody about the kind of rats I have. They are not real rats, he says, not the kind you find in Britain. They are almond rats, shy nocturnal creatures which live on a diet of almonds and are so timid they will never, ever come in the house. I must not 'vorry'. He will be back in a few days with his team of men to point the stone at the front of the house and 'We will forget about the rats.'

Wagtails are busy flipping grubs, blackbirds and robins are rummaging in the acid yellow flowers of the alfalfa which has sprung up in dense clumps in the field and I need essentials from the village shop. I have a deep basket with leather straps hanging on an old farm implement behind the door – it has menacing metal spikes embedded in a plank of old pine and, hung up high on the wall, is perfect for hats and coats and things. It's also a bit lethal if I'm not careful.

The basket and I trip off down the road to my favourite *colmada* behind the church. Here Elena and her parents supply the village with everything, from oranges in season to freshly baked bread. Elena has long dark hair and is fiery. She's not yet twenty and keeps a firm eye on her father, any shirking and she bustles him up like a bee. Elena's father is one of two bakers in the village and spends long nights and sleep-filled days in his bakehouse next to the shop. Sometimes, particularly in the summer, the oven heat is so overwhelming customers have to shake him awake if they want to buy bread. He is a kind man, who'll shrug a little and smile at the inconvenience of being caught nodding off. There are not many who can stand the dual heat of an oven and a hot humid summer and I sometimes wonder whether the villagers really appreciate this treasure in their midst. It won't be long before the big bakeries take over, I'm sure.

The shop, where all the womenfolk of the village gather to chat, is long and narrow and also stifling hot in summer, protected against flies with long strands of silver chain at the door which tinkle when a customer comes in. The boxes of fresh fruit and vegetables are stacked so I'm able to dive in and help myself, local tomatoes, mushrooms, plums in season, anything grown in the district is sold here along with produce picked up every other day by Elena from the teeming Mercat Olivar, the main market in Palma. There is always a leg of ham on display, ready to be carved, and whole Manchego cheeses, but I have to arrive early if I want to get served quickly. Being polite is a bit risky. If I let one of the local ladies in before me I'll be there most of the morning as she goes over every piece of fruit or remembers, just as I think she's on her way out the door, to pass on a particularly juicy bit of gossip to whoever else is in the shop.

Today, I'm in luck, the *colmada* is empty, it is deliciously cool and I am in and out with bread and enough tomatoes and oranges to last a week. I've been told the best oranges are those grown in *tierra roja*, the red earth around the towns of Santa Maria and Manacor in the middle of the island, as they're sweeter than those grown in the *tierra blanca* of Soller and Deia on the coast. I'm not sure I can yet tell the difference, all I know is that they are at their juiciest just now and Elena has tubs full.

The Tabac – or tobacconist – in the square sells the local

English newspaper, the *Majorca Daily Bulletin*, along with pencils and paper and stamps. Today, the front page is filled with a poor forecast for the tourist season and a list of local markets. I pull off a chunk of still warm bread and read the weather is set to be fair for the rest of the month. Which is all I need to be happy.

The next few days are spent picking big yellow mushrooms in the fields and planning which bits of the house I want to have restored. Like the dunny, for example, which is claustrophobic and smells mousy. I'm learning more about Boris and how brilliant he is at transforming old fincas with his artist's eye for the romance and antiquity of a place so I hope he might also makeover the bathroom, which is about to part company from the rest of the house, so big is the crack through which I can now definitely see daylight.

I have no inclination, in my daydreams, to consider the odd behaviour of my neighbours, although I notice Francine, Gunther's wife, is not acknowledging me if our cars pass on the road. Apparently the Mallorquín way of greeting someone unknown is to tip the head back, raise the eyebrows and not smile to prevent any unwelcome intrusion. I am beginning to get used to Francine's adaptation of this admirable technique, which I've come round to believing saves a lot of energy. I think I smile too much after all those hours on the breakfast sofa greeting guests. It would be wonderful not to, sometimes, but if I'm serious about this I'm going to have to practise lifting my eyebrows a bit more meaningfully.

Francine has a thick mop of dark wavy hair, she's slim, has an aquiline profile and is also pretty nifty on her feet. She has a herd of goats which she rounds up by running up and down the hill, leaping sure-footedly from rock to rock, although I notice the goats make their own way home in single file to be milked by her at night, their bells reverberating in my sleep. Francine works diligently to produce soft bite-size cheeses for Gunther, which no one else gets much of a chance to taste. He swallows them whole. She keeps the goats, who keep down the scrub, just for him.

It's a dewy January morning when Boris and his building team decide they're going to begin work. Boris arrives first at half past eight in a rattling old Renault followed by Rafa, Mario, and Carlos buzzing behind on their mopeds. Rafa has vivid red hair, pale skin and is a dead ringer for that other redhead, Jaime I. Rafa really does look like the statue of the conqueror on his horse adorning the main square, the Plaza d'Espana in Palma; he has a powerful upper body which is just as well because Rafa is also Boris's labourer.

His other worker, tall, supple, dark-eyed Mario, fled from his home on mainland Spain when a nuclear power plant went up nearby and has not gone back, preferring to stay on the island and toil, although gardening is his first love. Mario will tenderly move even a weed to a safer place if he thinks it's going to get squashed by a JCB, a rare and remarkable thing in a builder.

And Carlos with his sweet face and flat cap is introduced

as Boris's cement expert. It will take a while for me to understand there's a skill to laying cement in Mallorca where even for the smallest job extra thickness and extra reinforcement is essential because the earth expands and contracts so forcefully in the heat. Carlos attempts to keep Boris right, as the artist in Boris will happily slap earth-coloured Mallorquín cement, freehand, on almost every wall if he can get away with it.

This morning, perhaps because it's damp, the genny jibs a bit but soon, with a little coaxing from the choke, a purring and then a chugging gets the gang underway and I am despatched to Andratx to pick up enough fuel to last a week.

The market town of Andratx with its grid of sunburned terraced houses concertinaed in streets laid out over a thousand years ago, is still trim and interesting. Dominated by its great church and an imposing castle, there are bakeries on almost every corner, cool courtyards behind high garden walls, polished brass on oiled pine front doors; it hasn't changed much since Ludwig Salvator, an Austrian archduke, left Viennese court life behind to settle in Mallorca. 'Andratx, Roman Andrachium,' he wrote in 1867, 'is inhabited mostly by seafarers and shows kindness and prosperity to quite a special degree. Happy, content faces smile at the onlooker from every house; it is just one of those places where anyone would be glad to settle.'

I bet generations of Mallorquíns have been grateful to bed down here at the foot of its mountain, Puig de Galatzo, protected a little from pirates who came ashore at the port three miles down the road to murder and massacre and take into slavery anyone left standing. A particularly brutal raid by bandits from the Barbary Coast in 1553 is still vividly remembered by townspeople who dress up as Moors and Christians every August to re-enact their 450-year-old battle. As always, the Christians win.

Unspoiled towns like Andratx are forever under siege. It's hard, on this January morning, to believe that having got almost to the end of the twentieth century in such fine shape Andratx won't look like this much longer. In the years ahead a local mayor and his planning officer will be caught and sent to gaol, but not before large chunks of the old town have been destroyed and ugly and incongruous apartment blocks have been given the go-ahead like bad teeth in a once perfect smile.

The Andratx wisteria – one of the finest specimens I have ever seen in the centre of the town – will go the same way, eventually being cut down to make way for a savings bank. It smothers a coffee bar now, on the corner where the weekly market meets each Wednesday, twisting its way round street lanterns and electricity wires all the way up the road. In spring its pure, delicious purple attracts hundreds of bees, today it's getting an annual trim from a group of fellows wobbling volubly on step-ladders. I make a note that I should certainly find a place at my house to plant a wisteria like this as it obviously loves the climate so much.

When I get back to the house with my haul of fuel there's

much muttering going on. The men have stopped work. Lauren, I see, has turned up and is talking to Boris who looks sheepish. 'Er, I have news for you,' he blusters as I stagger up the stone steps with the petrol, 'Ve have no generator. It has gone.'

'Gone, where's it gone?'

'Johnny has taken it. He came up here half an hour ago and says it's his and he vants it back.'

'And you let him just take it?'

'Vell, it vas his.'

Lauren quickly says she can't offer me hers because she needs it.

'But why on earth would Johnny want his old genny back?' I demand to know, fuming now. 'A machine which is absolutely essential to the running of this wreck of a house...' and then, 'I thought, in any case, he was supposed to be going back to the UK?'

All four guys look at the ground for any sliver of inspiration as I rant on about how mean and miserable can a person get, to come and nick a sodding generator. Or words to that effect.

Mario then does the only thing reasonable under the circumstances – he offers to go and borrow one until I am able to find a replacement. In other words, he's outta here. Which leaves me with the others, Carlos and Rafa, who grab their baskets with fruit and water and go squat near the bread oven to have their lunch.

Boris and Lauren don't bother to try and placate me, it's obvious this is the kind of behaviour they're used to. Lauren, in any case, has come to see if she might nick Boris for an hour or so to fix her water pump but before he slinks off to help her, I want to know the form. How come Boris gave in so willingly to Johnny when I'm the one paying the wages?

Lauren says they all go back a long way because, for God's sake, they all arrived together, but before she can fill me in, Boris quickly changes tack. He's looking worried. 'Let's forget about Johnny,' he says. 'Ve have plenty of work to do and Mario vill find another generator.'

Lauren shrugs as Boris prattles on about how he can envisage a lovely iron trellis at the front of the house to carry the vine now threatening to squash the makeshift structure it currently leans on. 'Ve von't need a generator for that, vill ve?' he says, hoping to flatten my rage.

Lauren meanwhile has spotted an opportunity to inflict one of her crushing bon mots instead.

'What you need to realise, if you want to understand Boris is this,' she drawls, turning to me, 'there are two Germans in this valley who were once friends. One is Gunther,' she nods in the direction of Gunther's house, 'and the other is Boris. One is a neurotic,' Lauren pauses, 'and the other a psychotic.'

For a second I consider which one might best fit the bill but Boris beats me to it.

'And vich von am I?' he asks anxiously, giving the game away.

The rest of the day is spent hacking loose lime plaster from between the stones, so that by nightfall Boris's team have covered everything in yellow dust. Mario has returned, happy at finding someone prepared to lend a generator, and Boris has got over his neuroses to stay and talk me through the intricacies of choosing the right model. The conversation kicks off okay but then, as he starts getting technical about voltage and power surges and whether diesel or petrol is best, I start feeling low and as the light fades Boris delivers his own *coup de grâce*. 'Ve von't find a genny in Mallorca built to last. Best bring one out from Britain.' I'm ready to pack it in.

By next morning, after a blissful sleep, things look different. It can't be that difficult to get my hands on a generator. After all, the island resounds with the unrelenting din of them. As I make my way downstairs, treading barefoot on the tiles to boil a kettle, I notice there's half a lemon lying, once again, on the kitchen floor. The lemon is a bit odd. I can't work out how it's got there two mornings running, but there's enough left on the worktop to salvage a slice for my tea before the men arrive and I can go on the hunt for a new generator.

I've decided to start in Port d'Andratx, which is a mecca for yachties, men who spend hours mending and tending their boats hoisted high on platforms in the harbour. If there's any place where I can find someone who knows about engines then this is it. The port has a unkemptness to it still, a sprawling reed bed filled with wildlife stretches from the sea towards the hills which descend as steep and treacherous cliffs. It is all very beautiful.

This morning the fishing fleet has landed and their catch off-loaded so there is much breakfast merriment in the café close to the harbour. English holidaymakers are arriving in small groups off buses, strolling along the shore as I head to the Café Consignia for coffee and fresh orange to plot my next move.

There's a local paper left on one of the tables which has a story about Claudia Schiffer having problems with a photographer in the port. I think I've seen him on his rounds. He rides a scooter, has a pock-marked face, lumpy nose, thick glasses and curls anchored under a baseball hat. Very fetching. He puts on a show of pretending he's not looking for a photo opportunity but either he or one of his mates managed to climb a high wall to grab pictures of Claudia, topless, in her parents' swimming pool and Claudia's now complaining that a lucrative advertising contract is under threat because she has been seen semi-naked in magazines round the world. I feel sorry for Claudia, it's gut-wrenching to have snatched photographs taken in private moments, but I'm not in the mood to dwell too much on her plight, feeling lucky that somehow I've managed to dodge whatever press interest there might be in me by decamping to a rough house up a rough track where I can happily do simple things without being watched. It is a real joy and one I don't want to ever have to think too hard about.

A loud voice interrupts my thoughts. 'Hello, what are you doing here?'

I'm about to pretend it's not me when, 'Selina, it's Joe' breaks through. It's an Irish friend of mine who I haven't seen for years, pulling up a chair. Joe is a musician who spends most of his time touring Europe, so I shouldn't be totally surprised to see him in Mallorca, but to run into him in the port is quite a coincidence because one of Joe's great loves in life, apart from music, is engines. He couldn't have turned up at a better time.

Having got a willing Joe on the track of a generator, I am able to return to the house to check on Boris and his boys, stopping to talk for a few minutes with Kendi, who cocks her head from one side to the other as I tell her how lovely she is and how clever. I so want her off the chain, walking with me, and I know she craves the same but there are moments like this when I can't see how it'll ever happen. It's hard not to feel despondent as I leave her behind, cramped and chained.

'What's a bar of soap doing on the kitchen floor?' I ask of Boris who's up a ladder hacking away with a hammer and chisel. The soap has got me momentarily foxed. When I bend to pick it up I can see what look like teeth marks etched into its softness and it dawns on me that far from rats 'never ever coming in the house' they are already firmly in residence, making themselves completely at home with my lemons and my soap.

'Boris!' I yell.

Boris, who'd been expecting a warm *buenos días* from me, trips down the ladder. 'What's this?' I shove the soap at him. Boris forces a wan smile and says what I need is a cat to come and live with me.

The hunt for the rats goes on for an hour before the pantry is universally declared their hidey-hole even though there isn't any sight of them and no one can figure out how they're getting in. The cracks in the bathroom wall are deemed too narrow for a big almond rat to squeeze through so I am left on my own in the house, on guard.

In the meantime Joe has done a great job. He's found a monster of a generator – nearly new – at a boatyard in the port which he's having delivered on the back of a big truck. There are smiles all round as the bright red machine is winched off and wheeled into my sitting room for safety. Now we have to find it a home of its own, so Boris diverts his men off the stonework to begin a new project: restructuring the dunny ready for its new inhabitant.

'You know, when you see pictures of life in remote villages in India,' Joe muses, while Boris and his gang get into gear, 'there's always a light bulb hanging up there.'

He has a point. Poor countries in the Third World have electricity, so why not a country home in Spain, a burgeoning and soon to be member of the new European single market? I know that the state-owned electricity company Gesa, with its total monopoly of the market, has no interest in houses like mine. It has to keep power surging through under-ocean electricity lines or so it tells us. More likely it has no time for houses owned by foreigners. An attitude that takes some getting used to.

Joe says he has to be going, he's only come to Mallorca for a few days before a concert tour of Germany but he'll keep in touch and hope I manage with my new toy. I thank him profusely and go straight back to initiate another major search of the house for my elusive almond rats.

Later that day after Boris has gone and the peace of a sunny evening descends, great sobs ricochet through the air. At first I can't make out where they're coming from but a moment later Emmy Lou turns up, tears tumbling. I haven't seen her since we drilled for water but something must be terribly wrong for her to be like this. 'What is it, Emmy Lou?' All she says is she 'had to do it', her shoulders heaving with the effort. This is beginning to sound bad so I find a chair and a glass of wine and try and calm her but she is inconsolable.

Eventually, as the light dips she tells me in a muffled voice she has had a terrible decision to make: she has had to kill the cats. She says it's all her fault. 'I shouldn't have brought food up from the village but I can't just leave them all to starve.'

It transpires Emmy Lou has to go to the States for a few months and she has been beside herself over what to do with the cats she has encouraged into the valley. Her anguish has coincided with the arrival of two young German vets on the island who are planning to humanely destroy dozens of poor creatures who'll be left with nothing to eat when the cafés close for the winter in San Telm, so Emmy Lou had asked if they would come and do the same to her cats here.

'No one understands,' Emmy Lou sobs. 'Carter is calling me a murderer and now I don't know where Tiddles is. She ran away when all this started.'

I feel desperate for her and tell her it's the kindest thing she could have done and that I'm sure Tiddles will return, but of course it's all so horrendous for Emmy Lou and for me, too, for that matter. What an awful end to another lovely day.

three

A whistle pierces the morning haze. My film crew, who until then have been desultorily chatting to one another, suddenly jump. We have been waiting in the courtyard of the Alcazar Palace in Seville for His Majesty King Juan Carlos of Spain to begin his tour of the city and the heat is building.

Security guards ease out of the shadows, chauffeurs in wrap-around sunglasses nervously tug at the doors of their black limousines, as another whistle and 'Selina!' lobs sexily through the stillness, down from an ornate balcony on high. Juan Carlos is waving. My cameraman, dashing Steve from Birmingham, thinks the King is calling him so grins and waves back, missing the moment, of course, to capture on camera this most informal of monarchs at his most mischievous.

It had been quite a challenge to get Juan Carlos and his Spanish advisors to agree to the documentary. Spaniards are not encouraged to get up close and personal with their King especially on TV. The old guard at the Zarzuela Palace in Madrid made sure the royal mystique, if that's what it can be called, dripped on its loyal subjects only at chosen moments. This was still a young monarchy in a new and potentially volatile democracy. The dictator, Francisco Franco, who died in 1975, had picked Juan Carlos to succeed him. Rocketed out of exile, Juan Carlos helped propel Spain, once considered Europe's Third World backwater, to prosperity. Integration into the European single market and ten years of stable socialist government under Felipe Gonzales had culminated, in 1992, in what promised to be a spectacular year for the country.

The bold gamble of staging both the Olympic Games in Barcelona and the Expo in Seville in the one year had sparked the world's interest. How better, I gamely thought, to celebrate this Year of Spain than to ask if I might make a filmed profile of its popular King?

It helped that I had a pad in Mallorca. At least I was able to gauge, in a tiny way, the energy and enthusiasm coursing through the country. ITV back in the UK wasn't so fired. Letters went back and forth, me trying to persuade them that this would be a project with ratings assured, but TV execs appeared to be more interested in the football fixtures of the year than a film about some European royals. 'Who is this Prince of Spain anyway?' asked a commissioning editor in the middle of a particularly fraught meeting. Er, actually he's a king, not a prince, I spluttered.

Things were not going too well at the other end either. I had fixed up a meeting with the elderly men gate-keeping the King's office in Madrid. Zarzuela Palace, the surprisingly modern home of Juan Carlos, his wife Queen Sofia and their three children, is on the outskirts of the city, situated in the middle of a deer park parched with the Spanish sun. At the Zarzuela, I was greeted courteously but with as much enthusiasm as I'd encountered in London. The Spanish Court was not for budging. It didn't want the King to take part even though, I tried to reassure them, this would not be for domestic consumption. The King and his family would only be seen talking to me in English. I was shown, politely, the big brass-hinged door.

I got an unexpected breakthrough a few weeks later. There had apparently been a lot of discussion about my idea and many younger officials in the Palace were pressing for change. They wanted to see their King portrayed across Europe as a forward and modern monarch, at home with his people. I was summoned back to the Zarzuela, this time to meet Juan Carlos to see if we might agree terms. The room was richly furnished in mahogany and perfumed with Havana's best. King Juan Carlos, with loafered feet, leaned back in a high wing chair as I outlined the plot to his advisors and where I hoped we would film: Madrid, Barcelona, Seville, Extramadura and Mallorca. Finally, Juan Carlos, carefully mouthing cigar smoke towards the frescoed ceiling, said, yes, he would do this, on condition we spoke only in English and didn't mention Franco.

With the King on board, it was now vital ITV gave its backing. We had exclusive access; we would be the only film crew out of 10,000 journalists covering the Olympics to be allowed to accompany the royal party. Still, there was procrastination.

A deal was eventually struck with Grampian, one of the smaller companies in the ITV firmament which had been promised nationwide airtime on the network. As no one thought the film ('foreign'!) would get decent ratings, Grampian, being Scottish, went on a desperate trawl for a partner, a company that would help shoulder the financial burden, and came up with a new player on the media scene in Spain, a French cable company, who were looking to make a splash.

Our new partner was informed the King wouldn't, under any circumstances, speak Spanish on camera, that the UK had the first airing of the film and as executive producer, I was in charge. It meant I picked up another crew, an extra cameraman and assistant, Alberto and Paloma, along with a producer Nacho, who would be a godsend with translation and getting things done. They got second use of the film, subtitled, to play on cable – all sides happy at the outcome.

Through all the negotiations I was keen to make my off-the-beaten-track Mallorca a centrepiece of the movie, hoping that in appealing to an international audience there might still be time to protect the unspoiled island from overzealous developers already lining up to destroy it.

We began filming at the King's home in Madrid, where it soon became evident that here was someone ready to throw himself into the spirit of movie-making from the off. Anything we asked Juan Carlos to do, he did with enthusiasm, although at quite a pace, which is why I got caught out with him and his Harley Davidson.

We had heard that the King would often take off on his motorbike round the streets of Madrid, wearing a black crash helmet. There were numerous stories of how he'd stopped to offer his unsuspecting subjects a lift, or a helping hand. It was Juan Carlos's way of getting to know his country incognito. Eventually, of course, he'd lift his helmet and be recognised but the message was out: here was a young king, in touch with his people, raring to go.

Would his Majesty mind if we filmed him getting on his bike, riding off into the distance for one of our sequences? No problem. He waved to one of the royal mechanics to bring on the royal bike and a gleaming Harley was wheeled into shot. The King mounted it and turned the key to start the machine. Nothing happened. The camera was rolling and, knowing I might lose this opportunity if we didn't get the thing moving, I stepped forward and pointing to the choke, suggested, 'Sir, why not give it some gas?' Juan Carlos obliged and to my amazement, and his, the machine powered up, and roared off.

When the King on his bike came back into view I had already decided this might not look so clever on camera, me showing him, a monarch, how to start a motorbike. Would his

Majesty like to do the sequence again? No, no, he was absolutely positive, we had so many other things to do. Which was why, when the film finally aired, I got it in the neck from Spanish commentators who universally agreed I had portrayed their macho king as a bit of a fool. After all, every Spanish male knows how to start a motorbike, don't they?

After the motorbike came the helicopter. King Juan Carlos is also a helicopter pilot and wanted to fly us to a tiny hilltop monastery, where his grandfather Alfonso XIII sought refuge and solace after abdicating. It would be interesting, I thought, for us to talk to him about his family, the Bourbon kings, at this remote sanctuary.

Unfortunately we did the trip at such a gallop – and once at the monastery couldn't talk through the clatter of the blades of the helicopter – that my cameramen, despairing, never did capture a 'clean' shot, that is, a beginning, a middle and an end sequence that would allow the film editor back at base to cut and thread the pictures together. All we had which was in any way useable was a dramatic shot of Juan Carlos practically crash-landing the machine back in Madrid, in an avalanche of dust.

I blamed myself for not insisting the King slowed down, but in those early days of filming I wasn't quite sure what his reaction would be. He was obviously used to taking charge and impatient but the Spanish critics didn't cut me any slack on this either. How dare I portray their King as an incompetent at the controls of his helicopter?

I had a feeling these very human qualities of the King would go down well in the UK, which they did, but when the Spanish got their hands on my film (something I had not foreseen) well, then it was a different matter. Let's just say the British sense of humour in those days was not the same as the Spanish. In any case, the expensive and wasted day trip to the monastery focused me. I took the King aside and explained the difficulties we faced and from then on, having learned fast, Juan Carlos geared down. In the filming that followed the King instinctively knew when the camera was on him and how long we needed him to hold the shot. He suddenly turned completely professional.

Our great and unspoken difficulty was a man who had been dead seventeen years. Francisco Franco had the blood of millions of Spanish families on his hands. The last thing Juan Carlos wanted was to reopen the devastating wounds of the Civil War by discussing his relationship with Franco on TV, a man who had guided the young King's military education in order that he should succeed him as head of state.

Although no one spoke much about these things openly in Spain, tensions weren't far from the surface. Shots were fired in the Spanish parliament, the Cortes, only eleven years earlier while Juan Carlos was playing a game of squash. His decisiveness in appearing on national television to assert his authority was widely credited with defusing the attempted military coup.

In fact, Juan Carlos had scarcely put a foot wrong since

becoming monarch on Franco's death. Within three years he had overturned virtually everything Franco stood for and certainly over the past decade Spain had become the success story of Europe. It was obviously difficult for older Spanish commentators to have to watch the person who, they believed, had saved their democracy portrayed on TV in such a natural and, in their minds, disrespectful way. A mass ITV audience, on the other hand, wasn't into history lessons, wanting instead dollops of personality, glamour and action from a king whose country many had holidayed in. Which is what had also appealed to Juan Carlos. He would later tell me, 'We had this reputation as a country where everything could wait until tomorrow, the "*manana*" effect. Of course it was a myth, but the only way to prove that was to show the world how efficient we could be.'

I managed to get back to Mallorca, once our first tranche of filming was finished in Madrid, to check on my own efficient team of workmen. Unbelievably, my house had been transformed. Boris had turned out to be quite a craftsman with stone, making the miserable-looking dunny into a rustic work of art. The new generator, wired up, ready to go, sat smack in the middle of it, but all work had come to a stop, I was proudly informed, when Mario one morning spotted an almond rat reclining on my sofa, and they had all gone to find out how it got in, to finally solve the mystery.

The pipes behind the water tank held aloft on the platform in my bedroom had been its point of entry. Johnny had not cemented round the pipes when the tank was installed so there was a big hole exiting on to the roof. All the rats had to do was abseil down and, yippee, they were in. Mario had personally seen to it that there were no more rodents lurking in dark corners and the inside of my home was now, he could definitely guarantee, a rat-free zone.

After Madrid Mallorca took a little getting used to again, rats or no rats. Ten o'clock at night in the capital meant going out, eating or clubbing, not heading for bed by candlelight. Sleeping for Madrileños, I was astounded to discover, was from anywhere between three or four in the morning. How they managed to turn up for work at 8.30 and not indulge in a siesta in the afternoon was miraculous but Madrid, then, was full of verve. It was preening itself on being the European capital of culture and our media partners in Madrid were right on the beat, lunching us late with risotto and ceps, gilded bream and albarino wine in celebration.

Everywhere, it seemed, was charged, focused on catching up fast with Spain's more prosperous northern neighbours. Soon, this commercial dynamism would spread and catch on in places like Mallorca, but I did wonder when I returned that year to a building site in a valley on the edge of Europe what on earth I was actually doing there.

It wasn't helping that I had begun to take on responsibilities I shouldn't have. Like Jake, the grey-and-white kitten who'd come out of the *torrente* in the village one morning, introducing himself by dabbing his paw as I nibbled my ensaimada. We shared the breakfast pastry because he was very hungry and next morning, he was there again, but this time badly cut from fighting. One of his eyes had closed up, lumps of fur were missing and his nose was bloody. Did anyone own him? Blank looks all round. He was just another feral cat struggling for survival, so I purloined a box from the bar, shoved him in and carried him home. He screamed and spat all the way.

Rafa was leaning against the *cisterna*, idly waiting for Cedric the plumber to arrive, when Jake leapt out of the box and galloped for cover under the honeysuckle, his ears pinned to his head, terrified. 'He's here to help keep the rats down and you're going to help look after him.' I tried to sound assertive.

Boris, who had just emerged from the dunny, shook his head. 'He'll go straight back to the village,' he warned, 'this is not his territory and who's going to feed him ven you've gone?'

'The cat doesn't stand a chance,' I replied, 'with all the others fighting for scraps of food, and I'm sure Emmy Lou will feed him until I return. I can't see there'll be a problem especially as Jake can live in the bread oven, in a warm box with a cushion. At the very least, he'll frighten off rodents and keep you guys company.'

None of them appeared particularly impressed by this suggestion as Jake continued to cower under the honeysuckle. And then Cedric made an appearance. Here was another bundle of fun on the scene.

Cedric, a cockney whose blond beard disguises a mournful

demeanour, had come to discuss a new bathroom with Boris. Cedric is also an electrician and a man of many parts, having learned a very useful trade as a telephone engineer back in the UK. Cedric has been in and out of most homes in this part of the island to fix things and is well up on who is with who and what they get up to together. He isn't given to being loquacious, he doesn't need to be, because Dottie, who he lives with, has it all clocked. Dottie, with her blonde curls, has two children with Cedric, and together they embrace village life, which means being regulars at both bars, observing all that goes on in them. Dottie, therefore, is a joy to talk to.

While the men discussed the septic tank, a rain cloud came over and poured down. I was in the sitting room when Jake gave up his sulk and shot out, wet through, from under the bush landing smack in the middle of my feather-cushioned sofa. He looked like a cat with a good eye on a mission. He had decided, I think, to stay.

His wounds healed and soon Jake and I settled into a routine. I was determined he would live outside, he was even more intent on being in. He ingratiated himself, following me around, watching with interest the comings and goings of the house. At night I would put him to bed in the bread oven but by next morning, he'd be hanging upside down from the guttering outside my bedroom window, tapping on the glass, miaowing for me to get up and let him in. Then he'd leap on my bed and as close to my ear as a cat like that can get, begin the mightiest purr. His oddest habit however was reserved for my feet. He loved nibbling my toes. Anyone's toes, actually, but mine in particular. I got so that it was always a dash in the morning to find shoes, otherwise if he got to my feet first he'd never let go.

I'd had a phone call from Joe a couple of days after Jake came to live with me wanting to know how I was coping with the new genny and reminding me that it would need a service before long. He'd had an idea. He could come and stay in the house when I was away filming and rig up a system that would store power in batteries. It would mean I wouldn't have to cart heavy gas bottles around and he could also service the generator while he was at it. He made it sound so easy and enticing, turning my house into a proper home, almost like being on the grid.

He also thought my place was heaven for children and would I mind if he brought his boys along too? Now this was something I hadn't anticipated. Mallorca was my bolthole not a holiday camp. Joe also had a complicated love life. His sons were from a previous marriage but he always seemed to have at least two women on the go at the same time, neither of whom knew about the other. I didn't want anything to do with his domestic arrangements but couldn't figure how I was going to get out of this innocent and, on the surface, kindly suggestion. I told him I'd think about it and hoped, somehow, he and his bright idea would simply go away.

———

It is a shimmering May morning, Cedric is under the sink, cursing at the rusted water pipe which has seized solid. Jake is wide-eyed, watching, so I reckon this is a good moment to go find a wisteria I've promised myself. The walk to the garden centre in the port is a bit of a hike, but blackbirds are busy nesting, clacking at one another across the field, and I have nothing urgent to do. The rain last week, I notice, has loosened one of the fence posts round Kendi's enclosure so it's leaning at an angle, ready to collapse. The old man is inspecting the damage as I wander by and wonder if this might be my opportunity to sneak in later when he's gone. I pretend I haven't noticed him.

Everywhere is very fresh and green, all the flowers are out, white and bright blue daisies, oranges still hanging from orchards in almost every back garden and in the garden centre there are more exotic, tantalising plants. Towering palms, luxuriant bougainvillea, mimosa, jasmine, all thriving in perfect condition, but a tiny lapse in watering once they're replanted in the tough old clay of my valley and they'll conk out and die. I have lost too many to be tempted today, but Boris has promised he will water a wisteria and wants me to find a scented brugmansia too. He's got just the spot for them.

As my plants tuck easily into a basket and are light, I've decided to follow the old road back, through what is known locally as L'Estret, the nightingale valley, which will take me a bit longer to get back to the village. The road is single track and veers around derelict *casitas*, full of potholes and blind bends.

A House in the High Hills

As I walk up the hill I notice there's a building set back off the road and somewhere near I can hear whimpering. It's a dog but as I can't see exactly where it is, I assume it's tied up somewhere, waiting for its owner to return. The crying drops a little but now it seems to be coming from inside the building, which is chained and padlocked. I can't find a window but I know for certain a dog is in there, trapped. I'll have to go and get help.

Luckily I catch Cedric as he's just getting in his truck to leave. He's a bit disgruntled because the problem with the pipe has meant he's late for his other appointments. I'm breathless with the fast hike up the hill. 'You must come and help break open a padlock on a *casita* down the road.'

'Jesus Christ,' he says, 'you must be joking.'

'But there's a dog shut up and it can't get out.'

Cedric doesn't show any emotion, just says, with a sigh, 'jump in'. It doesn't take long to get to the place and to wrench the padlock and hinge off the door, although he's lecturing me, all the while, on why you can't go breaking into other folk's property because 'we'll both be sent down'.

As the doors creak open, in the far corner, in the blackness of an empty building, a large dog is chained to the wall. There's an empty bowl lying close by. The dog is emaciated and frightened. 'Oh, Cedric,' I start to wobble, but he is matter of fact. 'Let's go and report this to the police in Andratx because we'll be done for stealing if we take him. In any case, the creep who's responsible will only get another dog if this one goes missing.'

At the police station we're given the sympathetic treatment, but basically they're not interested. Some locals protect their property by locking dogs in them, so what? They can only do anything if there is no food or water. They know who owns the dog because he lives locally, so Cedric insists, in Spanish, that they must go and sort him out. Meanwhile, we are given the name of a German woman who runs a small animal refuge in the town who the police say will come and take the dog while they deal with the owner.

It's dispiriting. The refuge is in a backstreet, its rooms packed with kittens in cages, the garden crammed with strays. I don't know how she doesn't go mad, but she says she is happy to help and comes with us to rescue the dog, which staggers out, meekly letting us lead him away.

Cedric tries a pep talk on the way back to the house. He has four dogs, all of them abandoned, two he found as puppies left at the side of the road. Emmy Lou picked up two pups thrown out at the local tip, he says. Everyone he knows has opened their home to unwanted dogs on the island. There's nothing else they can do. Lots of local people love their pets, he says, and the children at the school are being taught about animal welfare, so there is hope.

As Cedric leaves me at the bottom of the hill to walk on up, I can see Kendi through the hole in the fence. She's on her own, so, calling her name gently, I clamber through the gap into her enclosure. She starts to bark, one big woof followed by another, until I'm almost touching her. Suddenly she trys to bolt backwards, yanking her chain, afraid that I'm going to do something horrible to her. The best thing, I decide, is to crouch and keep on talking, carefully offering my hand, my palm up so that she can inch forward to investigate. Soon, she's crawling forward and I'm able to rub her soft brown head and her muzzle, as she makes funny little yelping noises of appreciation and starts peeing in spurts. I wish I'd brought something nice for her to eat but she doesn't seem to care. She's delirious at the attention she's getting. What I really want is to let her off the chain so she can stretch, although it crosses my mind she might take off and I'll never see her again. But what the hell, after my miserable afternoon with the other dog in the *casita*, I unclip her collar and she's off, round and round the compound, her tail between her legs, leaping bushes, knocking over buckets, with a mad grin on her face.

She is getting too excited but still she keeps on going, making big circles with me the object of her joy. After about ten minutes, on her umpteenth pass, when I notice she's slowing a little, I call her and am amazed at how quickly she obeys, slinking towards me, her head down. To anchor a lovely dog like this is torture, but I tell her I'll see her again soon as I have to go, carefully over the fence and up to the house, not daring to glance back.

It's like stepping into a haven, walking into the old kitchen where Mario has left a fire burning in the iron stove. He's put a tumbet in the oven for me, a simple Mallorquín dish of fresh aubergine, tomatoes, onion and peppers cooked in layers in olive oil which will take a couple of hours to cook, so I've time to look at Boris's handiwork before the light disappears.

He has been busy. The ground has been cleared and tiles laid ready for an outdoor eating area which will have stone benches, a charcoal fire and a wisteria wrapped round. It is all very artistic and cosy and Jake thinks so too, leaping into one of his more appreciative pirouettes.

On a thorn in the thicket of the hill a small brown bird has started to sing. It's getting dark but its song is exquisite and haunting. It is a nightingale and soon another will break forth from another bush on the opposite hill, singing its heart out, higher and higher it lilts, until I can hardly bear any more.

We have come to Seville with the King and his entourage, just ahead of the heat, having filmed first in wild Extramadura, close to the border of Portugal, where the Conquistadores were born. This bunch of daring, desperate men left their isolated hilltop villages to conquer Peru and the Inca Empire. Spurred by their greed for gold, men like Pizarro and Cortes left Spain from the River Guadalquivir in Seville to return home with a new world and a taste for potatoes and peppers.

The creative tornado whirling through Spain has coincided with the five-hundred-year anniversary of Christopher Columbus's discovery of the Americas. It seems every pavement in Seville, the city from which Columbus sailed, is blue with the blown blossom off the jacarandas as the King arrives on this important anniversary to tour the city's latest prize, Expo. We are here to try and keep up.

Paloma, our sound recordist, is a gypsy girl from Seville. She has long dark hair, twinkling eyes and an effusive personality which is mostly kept in check by our handsome young cameraman, Alberto, who plugs into her sound gear and pulls her along behind him. I don't really know how much experience either of them has in TV production but they come as a team, determined not to let anything faze them. It probably helps that Paloma is half English – her last name is Dunne, her father having fallen in love with a flamenco dancer – because Paloma's passionate nature is tempered by her sense of the ridiculous.

My Spanish crew hasn't been scheduled to work the day the King whistles from the Alcazar Palace, but Paloma turns up anyway to help lug equipment and steer us round her home city. She's momentarily taken aback at the sight of Juan Carlos calling from on high, but then mirth breaks her face and she begins to laugh. I'm restless, checking my watch, ready to jump and go the moment the King strides out, while Paloma continues to guffaw. Suddenly the cars in the outer courtyard glide forward and we're after them, off to the cathedral of Santa Maria, the largest of all Roman Catholic cathedrals, where the King will take mass, and then on to the Universal Exposition – the World Expo – held in a gleaming white installation on the banks of the River Guadalquivir. It's a long, very hot day and we wrap only when the King finishes his tour.

Paloma, however, is not for stopping – she is set on taking us to see the other side of her city, across the new and cripplingly expensive Alamillo Bridge to a place called El Vacie, a shanty town, sinister and desperately poor. This is Spain's underbelly, filled with gypsies and dereliction.

That night as the sun goes down, Paloma manages to squeeze us into a small backstreet bar, for a little entertainment. Soon, nonchalantly, an Andulacian man and woman dressed in black, she with scuffed red shoes, start tapping as though they're unable to find the right rhythm on the floor of a makeshift platform and in moments they're off on the wildest flamenco I have ever seen, winding in all those watching, including Paloma, who shout and sway in perfect pitch, mimicking the beat in the bar.

It's obvious everyone here can dance flamenco, only waiting their turn to take to the stage and keep the night pulsing.

'Paloma, what was so funny this morning?' I manage to ask in a lull in the dance.

'Oh, it's only that it occurred to me that you and I were standing in the Patio de las Doncellas when the King whistled at us,' she grinned. I look blank. 'It means Courtyard of the Maidens,' she went on, 'the place where the Moors demanded one hundred virgins every year from the Christians as a gift. And there we were,' she grinned, 'just the two of us, all these years later.' And off she went, giggling again.

I needed to get back to Mallorca and to stand down the crew so that we'd get time to prepare before our next rendezvous at the Olympic games and Barcelona. Although I'd got clearance to follow the royals, I knew that in the oppressiveness of a Spanish summer in a city frantically trying to cope with an avalanche of visitors, this was not going to be the easiest of gigs. Crown Prince Felipe, the eldest son of Juan Carlos and Queen Sofia, had been chosen to lead the Spanish Olympic team into the Montjuic Stadium and security, particularly with the threat from Basque separatists, would be tight.

Back in Mallorca, meanwhile, Jake had been enjoying himself, getting out of bed late to join the builders for breakfast and then again lunch promptly at one for morsels of sobrasada sausage, a Mallorquín speciality. Boris persuaded Emmy Lou to come and feed Jake on the days they weren't there, so a very relaxed and happy cat was awaiting me on my return. I still hadn't decided, however, what to do about that other headache, Joe. I wasn't in any rush to install an all-singing all-dancing lighting system when this was summer and I was spending most of my time outdoors anyway. Winter would be different, but then that was a long time off and I certainly couldn't think about that just now. Joe could wait.

I had much more important things to do like organising Boris, who needed guidance. He'd packed up on the stonework at the front, because he was bored etching out the old lime mortar. Years of hot sun had penetrated the surface, he said, and it would be far easier to put his signature Mallorquín cement wash over the whole house to protect it from the elements. He would do a piece for my approval. When I got back from Seville the house looked just like a mud hut. 'No, no, it looks awful, Boris.' So Boris, mortified, had to switch on the genny and pressure-hose it off while Rafa carted away the debris. All in an uneasy silence.

By evening he'd perked up. 'Vill you come for supper tomorrow night?' asked Boris when all the rest had revved off on their bikes. 'Eloise wants to meet you and ve can talk about the house. I have an idea.'

Whenever Boris comes up with a new idea, I'm worried because I know he's worried. If things aren't going right, like a displacement activity, think of something else to do. But I was being curmudgeonly. I would love, I said, to come for dinner.

———

I've noticed in my field an explosion of blue chicory flowers opening and closing as the light comes and goes, the petals blue when the sky is blue and grey as it fades and gets dark. Everywhere feathery wild fennel sways high above the other grasses attracting swallowtail butterflies and, in clumps near the back door, wild spinach has taken a firm hold. I have a harvest out there, all I need is guidance on how to make these aromatic herbs do the bossa nova with one another.

Luckily it transpires Eloise, Boris's wife, is just the person to help me. She's Canadian, warm and petite, and met Boris backpacking in Ibiza. Together they live in an old Mallorquín house, so swathed in foliage you can hardly see in or out, which only adds to its cradle-like charm. They are so welcoming, the two of them, as I duck under a mimosa and lift the latch on an old door set into a high stone wall. Supper is going to be outside under the stars at an olive wood table which started out as an old door and had been rubbed for hours with bleach to lighten and then olive oil for shine, so the table glows under the low lamp light.

Bruce and Joleen, an Australian couple, and Hildegard, an elderly German lady, have also been invited. They are all great friends and come to Mallorca for only a few months each summer, Bruce and Joleen retreating to the Seychelles for the winter, and Hildegard to the Alps. There's a lot of discussion over eye-lifts done on the cheap in Mexico to which Bruce, as an international traveller, is giving some dedicated thought, having taken a fancy, apparently, to his appearance. Bruce is well built, has a confiding voice and a conspiratorial manner, so it doesn't surprise me that he has been married three times and Joleen is his fourth. I've already heard all about Bruce from Dottie. Bruce likes to mix and match his women, bringing them all together even though they probably loathe one another – he likes to think he is a lion with a pride and the village is his den. Bruce's former wives and girlfriends have all taken up residence over the years, in and around the place.

Maybe it's because of her accent, but Hildegard has a

haughtiness about her, talking to Bruce as though he's a wayward son, but strangely likeable in spite of it. She tells him it's time he had his eyes done.

Eloise, meanwhile, is bustling Boris into the kitchen, where she is dishing up a feast of Mallorquín delicacies, new potatoes from Sa Pobla, crayfish from the port, strawberries in season, but for me the star is her wild asparagus salad. She's picked all the ingredients herself and dressed them in a herb vinaigrette. But how do you set about finding wild asparagus? It is something I'm itching to know after seeing local people gathering armfuls out of the scrub. Whenever I've rummaged in the undergrowth, it's like the proverbial needle in a haystack. Impossible.

'Wild asparagus,' says Eloise, 'hides deep in the prickles of a fern-like plant. You have to part the plant, which is tough, and its spikes can tear your fingers, but you have to know what you're looking for before you can spot the new growth.'

I suddenly realise which plant she means. I've seen its fronds everywhere but thought it was a particularly pernicious weed. Now I know what to search for, tomorrow it's going to be my very first mission.

'And then all you do,' says Eloise, 'is drop it ever so briefly in a pan of slightly salted boiling water. It's out of this world.'

As the vino plonko flows in the warming night we get round to discussing the folk who live on my side of the hill. Gunther for starters. Eloise confirms Boris and Gunther were once great buddies and even took a cycling holiday together in the south of France. 'So what happened to the friendship?' I ask.

'Well, the problem is,' interjects Bruce, 'they're too similar. The same age, from similar backgrounds and each thinks he's right and the other is wrong.' Boris looks a bit miffed at this. 'And so the two of them spent most of their holiday arguing. If they got something as straightforward as a puncture, there'd be a tiff. Gunther would want to repair it his way, while Boris insisted on his. They once went to collect apples in an orchard and fell out over how the apples should be stacked. Needless to say, they packed up their holiday early and have never really made up since.'

'The thing is,' Eloise confides, trying to see the best in everyone, 'Gunther is very clever. He had an incredible education under the Third Reich.'

'Does that mean he was a Nazi?' Joleen asks in mock horror.

'Well, I don't know about that, but he learned to speak perfect English,' Eloise said, not to be deterred, 'from a tutor brought specially from England to Germany to teach him before the war. He has marmalade on his toast in the morning. He's also fluent in French and Spanish and in fact can turn his hand to most things.'

I'm savouring the thought of Gunther, one of the brightest and best of his generation, camped up beside me with his breakfast marmalade, when Boris quietly changes the subject. He wants to build some more walls round my house so that I can have another courtyard at the back and be totally private, he confides.

Bruce has overheard. 'Where have I heard that line before, Boris?' he laughs. 'You know Boris paints pictures which he flogs when he spots a chance?' continues Bruce mischievously. 'Well, he once did some building on Peter Ustinov's house in Andratx and Ustinov bought a lot of Boris's work. Boris thought he was on to such a good thing that when he'd finished the building he said to Ustinov he should have some more of his pictures. Ustinov in exasperation said, but Boris I have no more walls to hang your pictures. Boris wasn't to be defeated. "So, why don't I build you some more walls, then?" Ustinov went off and bought a boat instead.'

Everyone laughs. I feel sorry for Boris, so I say, 'Well, maybe we can talk about walls when you're next up at the house,' to which there's another bout of hilarity.

The seductive warmth of the island means I am able to walk anywhere at night in comfort, often with the bright light of a rising moon. Supper has been lovely and Kendi, I see, is quiet in her kennel although she stirs as I near to give me a welcoming woof. To my dismay, the fence, I notice, has been fixed, the barricade is back.

———

There's a particularly dapper little man who's always dressed in a suit and tie and lives in one of the magnificent art deco houses in the village. I think he must own a lot of property in the district which he rents out because he doesn't seem to have a job. He's in his sixties and spends his spare time burnishing his house, of which he is very proud.

Every spring the shutters are treated to a sparkling coat of red paint and whenever a corbel or pillar chips or cracks, he has stonemasons round to fix it. His wife, who often sits in a chair at one of the windows, appears older than him. He, however, is breezy and friendly and always stops to say hello. I am particularly interested in his patio garden. It is a work of traditional Mallorquín garden art laid out in squares in a Moorish design. There is an orange, tangerine and two lemon trees separated by blue mosaic paths which lead to an old stone well carved with a frieze of vines. A wrought-iron pagoda drips grapes both green and black. There is also a kumquat tree. The garden has a patina of tender carefulness.

Sometimes a daughter, distracted, will leave the house wearing little make-up. I sometimes read my newspaper on a bench nearby and wonder about her ambitions and why sometimes she appears downcast. Soon, I must remember to ask someone about this family.

It has started to rain and across the street Pepita from the bar is out in her back garden with a towel over her head. Her washing is still on the line, a row of espadrilles beginning to dribble and several pairs of knickers. Pepita has a punk taste in hair dye. Red has been a great favourite for quite a while, but the hairdresser, the *peluqueria*, in the village square is having a go with an odd shade of pink which I'm not sure suits her. Maybe it's her daughters, Pia and Sofia, who lead her into this kind of mischief. They are a close and loving family and I don't think their mother needs much encouragement to trot across the square one colour and return illuminated another.

As Pepita's well protected from the rain she's begun hunting snails amongst the roses and is obviously finding juicy specimens, because I can hear them plop into her bucket as she moves slightly stiffly along. She must have quite a haul by now, which she'll cook in garlic, the aroma wafting out and along the *torrente*, driving the cats wild. Later she'll dole out equal portions of leftovers near an old well at the bottom of her garden to half a dozen strays who've invited themselves over to hers for dinner.

I'm hanging around this early in the village because I need to exchange my empty gas bottles but the wagon is late. Sancho hasn't any spares tucked away in his backyard so I will just have to be patient because both my fridge and water heater need replenishing. Dottie, who has arrived and is waiting for Cedric, calls from her car, why don't we have coffee in Lorenzo's?

Dottie, her blonde curls in a wiggle, gives up the gossip at such a breathless pace you have to pay close attention. She's full of Cedric's latest disaster, which, as it happens, inadvertently involves Bruce too. Cedric had been called out to fix the plumbing, a blockage in a lavatory in a fancy apartment in the port. Bruce had gone along to see if he could lend a hand and to nose round. The apartment was at the top of the complex, one of fifty or so built in a pyramid, on the slope of a hill. The vital services – sewage, water and electricity – were ducted and interconnected, so Cedric sent Bruce with a powerful machine ready to exert pressure on the lavatory in the top apartment when he gave the go-ahead, while he, Cedric, checked the outflow at the bottom of the pile to make sure there wasn't any obstruction in the system lower down. Dottie by now is almost beside herself. Two maiden ladies, she goes on, were having breakfast on their terrace in one of the lower apartments when Cedric showed up with his bag of tools and set to, prising open a manhole cover just below their balcony. 'Well, you'll never guess what happened next,' says Dottie. 'Bruce, not thinking, switched on the machine up the hill, which sent the blockage with such force down the main pipe that it burst out at the bottom, rocketing from the manhole thirty feet into the air, showering both Cedric and the ladies having breakfast with the biggest load of you-know-what.'

Dottie is convulsed. 'I don't believe it,' I say, but Dottie is bent double with the awfulness of it all.

Just then, there's a commotion and the gas wagon finally arrives to obstruct the traffic while Paco, the driver, goes through his routine. He's out of the cab, unhinging chains holding the bottles, then with a hook on the end of a pole, he fluidly swings each bottle off the truck and on the pavement. Dottie and I have managed to finish our coffee just as he deposits his load. For some reason gas bottles are like gold dust. If you have any, you keep tight hold.

Luckily my car is within Paco's orbit so he offers to lift the bottles into the boot and soon, having waved goodbye to Dottie, I'm off back to the house weighed down with my vital cargo. Getting a new bottle to the fridge is strenuous stuff. First bend the knees, then lock on to the handles and, taking a deep intake of breath, strain and stagger to the appliance most in need. A satisfying hiss means the cap fits the bottle and has connected to the gas. We're in business. And this has to be done at least once a week. I'll be like the Incredible Hulk by the end of the summer.

four

Barcelona is heaving. Both my crews are wired ready to go but the crowds and clammy heat make progress slow. We are trying to film Antoni Gaudí's Sagrada Família, his unfinished cathedral, but half a dozen other TV crews – mainly, it seems to me, Japanese – keep getting in the way. The beggars on the dockside think Christmas has come as boats large and small pile in from the far horizon and in the maelstrom King Juan Carlos is holding a Heads of State dinner in one of Barcelona's grander hotels. We are slated to be there at six. Juan Carlos is pleased to see us and, with his arm around Fidel Castro, immediately comes over and says, 'Fidel, meet my friend Selina,' which, of course, does for my impartiality.

Castro is dressed simply in a dark tunic with epaulettes and a serious cravat. He beams broadly as we are introduced. I can't believe I'm talking to the man who helped bring the world to the brink of nuclear war thirty years ago, a man who's squared up to eight American presidents so far and seen them all off. Now he's focused on something I'm saying and I'm aware how imposing he is, a well-built man, the same height as Juan Carlos. I need to film them, he and the King behaving like brothers, clasping one another, talking close, a demonstration of male bonding I know Juan Carlos is keen to portray, symbolic of Spain's new relationship with her former dependencies, a partnership of equals.

Watching Castro that evening, joking and engaging with the King, I wasn't a bit surprised to learn that after the Olympics he made an emotional pilgrimage to the village of Láncara in Galicia, where his father was born in a one-roomed house. Ángel Castro emigrated to Cuba in 1902, ninety years ago, and always dreamed of returning home. He never did. His son, Fidel, had to make the journey for him.

Another famous son, Prince Felipe, demonstrated his own filial pride the night the Spanish team marched into the Olympic stadium with him at its head. It was a quiet defining moment in the fevered atmosphere of the opening ceremony. Holding aloft his country's flag, Felipe turned and saluted his father and mother, Queen Sofia. Caught on camera, in the royal box his oldest sister, Elena, began to cry.

Meanwhile, like Cinderella, I have to flee the party early to make sure of a bed for the night. ITV had taken so long to sign up to the deal that every single room in the city has been booked. Somehow, we've managed to find a guest house in a run-down suburb which has enough space to just about accommodate us all and I've been given the best of it. I have a single bed with a light hanging from the ceiling and a cupboard with a bath you could just about sit in if you crouch. There is no air-conditioning and the place smells rancid. The guys have similar rooms, slightly smaller, which leaves Paloma and Alberto having to share a closet with only a couple of camp beds and no loo.

Steve, the cameraman, gallantly offers his room to Paloma, but she take one glance at it and shaking her head sums it all up in her best English: 'No, no, Steve,' she said, 'it's steell sheet, only bee-gger sheet.'

———

After the Olympics, the crew fly home for a few days' break while I decide to take the overnight ferry to Palma, to be there before the Royals arrive for their longed-for holiday after the excitement of the Games.

The Transmediterranea boat leaves at midnight from a berth in the heart of Barcelona so all I need do is turn up and buy a ticket. The cavernous booking hall has the feel of the 1930s about it and appears impressively well organised with dozens of windows marked with letters of the alphabet, but an hour before departure there's still no clue where in all this I should start queueing. Travellers keep arriving, aimlessly pacing the great tiled hall while they wait for the night's business to begin. Suddenly a window lifts and there's a stampede, but it turns out this is for Spanish residents only, who get a cheaper deal.

Cleaners with buckets of disinfectant mop up round feet and bags, and then another queue forms and this time it's for real. Although not one cashier has a word of English and there's much fumbling with pesetas, somehow through the chaos we all manage to board the boat on time, trooping up the steps, dozens of backpackers making a mad rush to be first for the benches on the deck.

I've bought a cabin for the crossing down several flights of steps. Julio Iglesias pipes me to my bunk but as there's still a few minutes before we sail, I'm soon back on deck to watch our departure. The bar is, by now, filling with truck drivers, sleeping bags unrolled, while onshore families are building to wave their goodbyes. As the ferry pulls gently away, there's a sudden tug, the ropes are winched and then, almost as an afterthought, the night ship emits a huge hoot: we're off.

My sleep, to the throb of engines, is fitful but the crossing is smooth and soon I'm awake, refreshed and on deck at dawn with a cup of tea, ready for our arrival into Palma. The Mediterranean on an early morning in summer is almost ethereal, the grey ocean slowly waking to a dreamy azure day. In the far distance, the glow of the golden stone of Palma's cathedral can just be made out, it looks like an upturned boat from here, a commanding sight that has inspired seafarers over the centuries.

By nine, we've docked and everyone's off at great and

happy speed. I manage to grab a taxi and head west, the whole day ahead of me. I'm looking forward to seeing what Boris and the boys have been up to. As always, I am deposited with my gear at the bottom of the hill as the taxi cannot – and will not – clamber up my road and I prepare myself to confront Kendi once again. Except today she's not there. Her chain is on the ground so perhaps, I psych myself, the old man has come in early and taken her for a walk before the day becomes too hot. I'll probably pass her on the way up.

By the time I finally reach the welcome shade of the pine trees I have not run into Kendi, but I can hear Boris, Cedric and the gang whistling and shouting. They've fixed the bathroom so it's no longer a break-away zone and have nearly completed my courtyard, an enticingly private place which incorporates an old stone staircase leading up to a first-floor balcony. The wisteria has been planted and tied to the railings, it's all very *Romeo and Juliet*.

Jake is delirious, purring and curling round my legs and Boris straight away wants to know about the wall. Do I want him to start now? It will wrap the house and give me total privacy. Maybe soon, I stall. Right now I have to concentrate on finishing my film, I can't be sidetracked by anything else. Would he mind coming back after the summer so we can talk again? Boris says that's fine by him.

Which is lovely, because it gives me time to myself.

Later that day the guys tidy up and leave me with detailed instructions on how to handle the genny so it will keep me topped up with water over summer. I assure them I'll cope. I'll be living in the house through these next two months, which will give me a chance to get into the rhythm of what is now my new-ish home. I have mosquito blinds in my bedrooms and a sense of seclusion. I'll be able to go filming with a king and get a suntan.

———

Jake is growing into a glossy young cat and, I notice, has started casing the hoopoe birds nesting in the hedge. His lurking is getting him into trouble. He doesn't like it when an adult swoops out screeching at him to clear off. They're big birds for a little cat, with bright plumage and sharp, piercing beaks, so he'll somersault and turn inside out, do anything, to duck and race back up to the house. He's on one of these fast getaways when Lauren arrives to talk about bringing electricity to the valley. She's desperate to have power so she can rent out her house for more money and have an easier life. As I'm still smarting over the saga of the drilling I'm not in the best frame of mind to discuss another problem. She however is conciliatory and wants me to come in with her if she can put a project together. It will mean her researching the line the electricity will take from the main transformer and getting permission from the owners of the land where the line will cross. It sounds like a lot of work. She is also going to insist, she tells me, on pinewood poles to carry the line rather than ugly concrete ones, so that electricity won't despoil our valley.

I want to know if everyone else is in agreement. Lauren says she knows Gunther won't want it, he won't pay, neither will Emmy Lou, so we will have to continue to put up with the noise pollution from their generators but there are others who want this as much as we do so we won't be on our own.

The prospect of ending my relationship with my new generator is enough for me. Yes, I say. Count me in. 'And by the way,' I ask as Lauren heads to the gate, 'have you seen Kendi recently?'

Lauren looks pained. 'Yes, unfortunately she's locked up in the shed.'

'But why?'

'She's on heat,' says Lauren, 'and to stop dogs getting to her, they've shut her in.' Lauren quietly closes the gate and leaves.

That night Joe's on the phone again, wanting to know if he can come and stay in August. It's impossible – I am in the middle of filming my documentary with King Juan Carlos – so Joe rings off saying he'll contact me again after it's finished. Which is a big relief.

Next morning, I do as I'm told and prime the generator before pulling the cord to let it run for at least a couple of hours to pump water. I'm not in the mood to hang around so, keeping fingers crossed it won't blow up in my absence, I set off for the village. There's a joy to tripping along dry dusty tracks in sandals and Jake is of the same frame of mind. He has begun accompanying me, striding along like a little dog, sometimes accidentally catching my heel with his paw, but he's not for going far. He'll stick with me to the third bend and leap on the bank, loitering there until I return. His kittenish ways always make me smile.

Three old men who once worked the fields are in Sancho's bar at their favourite table. I guess they're in their eighties: José with his rakish black beret is small and puckish, Mateo sports a red baseball cap while Juan always looks as though he's preparing himself for bad news. They seem content with one another's company although I gather they live alone in homes along the main road and have little money to spend. Apart from their bright hats, they're usually dressed in shabby grey trousers and grubby shirts but Sancho keeps an eye on them, not minding that they commandeer one of his best tables at the back of the bar. Sometimes they talk about the Franco years and get very animated, at others, like now, they sit quietly and watch the regulars come and go. José raises a glass of San Miguel beer, which he'll spin out all morning, and smiles, wishing me a Mallorquín *Bon Dia*. He is cheery but then Spain still includes its old people in daily life, which means old men and the odd dog are welcome to sit for hours in village bars.

Dottie is talking to a young man with a walking stick whose hand is wrapped in a woollen mitten. She introduces him as Nico. I know immediately who he is. 'You're Kendi's owner.'

'Yes,' he asserts, proudly.

He is a good-looking boy who is keen to show off his English.

116

'She is a lovely dog,' I say.

He agrees. 'Yes, yes, she's super, a super dog.'

'Where is she? She wasn't there this morning.'

Sombrely he nods and says, '*Sí*, Kendi, she quiet because of the *machos*.'

'But she's cooped up, isn't it too hot for her?'

'No. Kendi, she *comprende*,' he tells me authoritatively.

'You mean, she knows she's on heat and has to be shut up?' I try not to sound challenging.

'*Sí*.'

Dottie is grimacing and starts talking about how the summer is '*mucho calor*', very hot, until Nico decides to go, waving happily. This is impossible, and Dottie agrees, but says it's no use criticising as it will only get his back up and make it worse. Wonderful.

I have to go to the bank to pick up some pesetas, trying to work out how I can communicate better with Nico. The bank has a notice outside saying 'Caja de Ahorros', which actually means savings bank, but is known locally as 'The Cage of Horrors'. Inside, the manager, a plump pleasant fellow in his late fifties, counts thousand-peseta banknotes with long, dirty fingernails. He looks a bit down on his luck, but in fact he's up on everyone's affairs and nods knowingly before pronouncing on important financial transactions to those perched on benches, waiting. He is always pleased to see me, enunciating 'Selina' carefully as though he's picked up a whole new language with just the one word.

This morning, luckily, I don't have to spend long because there's no one in before me: like the shop the bank is maddening if other customers nip in especially as no one ever gets round to money matters straight away, finding out first how wives, daughters, granddaughters and cousins several times removed are faring before commenting on the state of one another's health.

In any case the generator is beginning to bother me. It worries me to leave an engine running when I'm not there to check up on it, although everyone else, it seems, leaves theirs while they get on with the rest of their day. A genny will splutter and soon a dozen more will join in, seemingly on the principle that a rattling ear splitter is better than a low just-audible rumble, so at least we're all in the same noisy boat together.

By the time I reach the road to the house, Jake's already been waiting for more than an hour and is cross, leaping out in front of me, as if to say, come on, what's kept you? I'm relieved to hear the genny has stopped because it's run out of fuel but until it's cooled down I'm terrified to touch it in case I spark the petrol. Oh, what heaven it would be to have electricity.

———

As my camera crews are about to descend to resume filming the Royals, it's a good excuse to go to Palma. I've booked a table at the Parlement, a restaurant close to the cathedral, so we can all catch up and be briefed. The Parlement is a favourite, a restaurant where paella, normally a lunch dish, is served for dinner on white linen tablecloths under crystal chandeliers in the grand Spanish tradition. The owner, Bernardo, is behind the long liquor-filled mahogany bar when we arrive and greets us warmly before nodding over to his waiters, all middle-aged, to show us to our table. There's an opaque glass panel at the back of the restaurant where a long table is laid for a dozen or more. A phalanx of severe-looking men in black suits arrive, trailing cigar smoke as they're ushered through. They're probably only local politicos here to hatch a deal, but the restaurant falls silent as they process past. It is all very melodramatic. So too, as it turns out, is my Spanish producer, Nacho, who has suddenly come over all pensive.

While the rest of the crew gobble plump fresh radishes and bread before cruising into gazpacho and then a platter of paella, Nacho continues to brood. He still hasn't lightened up by the pudding so now no one is in any doubt that Nacho, with his big brown eyes, is very troubled indeed.

He's under pressure, he says, because his bosses want the King to do some interviews in Spanish. They know we've got special access and are determined to get a bigger, Spanish piece of the action. I tell Nacho that this isn't on, it is certainly not part of the deal, and his bosses knew it when they signed up. Nacho then says if they don't get an interview they will walk away from the deal and he will lose face. Can't I just ask the King again if he will grant an interview in Spanish with him, before we leave Mallorca?

The last thing I need is a crew walk-out now so close to the finish of the film, so after a second or two I concur. 'Of course, Nacho, I will ask the King again,' I say knowing as we leave the restaurant and say goodnight, Nacho will never get what he wants.

———

We're all to meet at 9 a.m. at the Marivent Palace in a suburb of Palma. The gates are grand enough, set between two stone pillars in a long wall ringed with barbed wire close to the main road. It's easy to miss, there's a busy garage on the corner and a tattoo parlour close by, but once through the gates and along the curving drive it becomes more royal by the minute. There's uniformed staff everywhere. And security guards. A fine mist of water pulses over tropical plants in the grounds, leaving random refreshing puddles on the road as we arrive to begin work.

The Marivent is simple. A coolly tiled entrance hall leads straight into a large sunroom where a veranda with spectacular views of the Bay of Palma is furnished with sofas and photos and memorabilia. Amidst the many family pictures there's one of Diana and Charles and their two young sons happily smiling on the steps of the Marivent. The room is modern, designed for a slip-on way of life.

Queen Sofia in polo shirt, trousers and deck shoes dashes

off to organise orange juice because it is very warm and she guesses our camera crews must be thirsty. Sofia is a Greek princess who, like her husband, spent her formative years in exile worrying how to make ends meet and dependent on friends and relatives to offer a home. This perhaps helps explain her unaffected empathy. Sofia couldn't speak a word of Spanish when she married Juan Carlos but she has worked hard to win over the Spanish people with her warmth and dedication. Certainly the guys think she's the bee's knees to look after them like this.

Soon Juan Carlos is with us, and then their daughters, the Infantas Cristina and Elena. Both girls are obviously happy to have this family down-time after the Olympics but, still suffused with the excitement of Barcelona, they are keen to start prepping for another competition, the local Copa del Rey, The King's Cup yacht race, a sailing fixture staged every summer in the waters off Mallorca. Already there's feverish activity down the road in the Royal Yacht Club, the Real Club Náutico de Palma, as crews and boats make ready for the race. It's become a family affair, the King in competition with his son and two daughters, who spice up the opposition by skippering boats of their own. The King has a habit, however, of winning.

Our first filming gig is aboard the *Fortuna*, King Juan Carlos's speedboat, which is tied up in the naval yard close to one of Palma's busiest roads. Juan Carlos is keen to get going. The *Fortuna* is a sleek dark machine with its own skipper who has been with the King for years and knows where to go and how to get there fast.

Royal Standard flying, the skipper is at the wheel, the King next to him as *Fortuna* glides out from its berth using up a river of fuel. It never enters our minds how vulnerable we are as we surge out to sea. A few years from now, in 1995, a Basque sniper will be put on trial, captured by police as he prepared to kill Juan Carlos from an apartment overlooking the naval yard. On that morning, identical to this, Juan Carlos will be in the *Fortuna* as an assassin does a dummy run aiming to kill not just him but also the future Prime Minister José María Aznar. Juan Carlos was in the terrorist's telescopic gun sight three times that day. It was the closest ETA came to ending the life of the Spanish monarch.

We're speeding round the south coast of the island when the King decides he wants the wheel because we're not going fast enough. He's spotted a speedboat filled with paparazzi and wants to give them the slip. Soon two jagged rocks rear out of the water with a narrow gap between them. As the rocks get closer Juan Carlos opens the throttle, the boat lifts and, picking up speed, careers straight for them. I'm hoping my camera is focused because I'm not. Convinced he's going to misjudge the space and crash, I brace myself for the impact, but we whistle through, a cliff in touching distance either side. The King and his skipper glance at one another and grin. And the photographers confronted with the fastest jet-powered vessel in the Med don't stand an earthly.

A day at sea with Juan Carlos is certainly a spirited experience and by the time we get back to base he's still enthusiastically suggesting more. Would we like to take some shots of him on his motorbike, this time in Mallorca? I think it a good idea as we might then be able to dump the earlier, not so good, ones of him and me trying to start the machine. So after tea we progress to a quiet road on the coast, Juan Carlos on his bike, my cameraman riding pillion on another, hoping to follow the King and get a sequence on the move. It takes quite a time to load up the gear and for both bikes to get into synch but by then it's too late; Juan Carlos on his racer is not a slow mode kinda guy, he is bored, he's had enough. Next thing we know, the King shoots off leaving us to pack up and make our own way home.

Next day, as the crews have been assigned to follow and film the Royals at various official functions in Mallorca and I'm not needed, I pop into Port d'Andratx to reassure myself that things are going to plan. I want to film a cosy supper with Juan Carlos and his family and I hope that the small Mallorquín fish restaurant I've picked will be perfect. Eating away from Palma without the usual protocol is a regular holiday treat for the Royals but this dinner will be different. It has to be cleared with security, who are concerned there'll be a public scrum if word gets out. How to get cameras and lights into position without alerting the press will be a challenge, although I have asked that the Royal bodyguard be low-key when they check out the town. I've also sworn the restaurant to secrecy.

Today Port d'Andratx is beguiling. The dozens of small rowing boats tied to makeshift jetties hidden in the reeds of the water meadow are busy being made ready for a day's excursion. Juan St Juan, who owns the Miramar restaurant where the Royals will eat, knows the trawler fishermen well and so has the pick of the best fish, which he serves at smart tables under a colourful awning on the sea front. The Miramar is one of several fish restaurants in the port but Juan, who is Mallorquín, oversees an old established family enterprise that has been engaged in the business of cooking for generations.

Juan is slim and tall and when we meet to discuss practicalities, he's tense at being chosen to prepare supper for a king. His king. He's been told it could all go very wrong if too many people hear about it so he conducts our meeting at a whisper, his eyes darting back and forth, sensing conspiracy round every corner. Security guards, he confides, have been all through his restaurant, the kitchen, upstairs, out along the harbour, to check their positions on the night. He hopes no one has seen them, but he can't be certain; he's told his staff and the band not to breathe a word. A group of local musicians have been booked to sing Mallorquín songs through dinner, which all sounds lovely but I'm not sure is going to work on the night. Juan Carlos doesn't like music when he's eating, especially if conversation is in danger of being drowned out. It will, however, give the film colour and movement and I'm keeping fingers crossed the King will approve, but the more I hear from Juan about who's in the band and who they're related to, the more convinced I am that the entire port is now in on our secret.

We have several days more filming before we get to Juan and I'm worried that by the time we're ready for him he'll be done in by the strain of his subterfuge. Juan pulls himself up, however, straightens his shoulders and announces he will cope, '*no problemas*' at all.

————

Elena in the *colmada* back in the village has ripe watermelon, *sandia*, on the counter and slices me a delicious, dripping wedge for my walk home. There's no Kendi, only a few squawking sparrows bathing in the dusty road as I trudge to the top.

Lauren collars me just after I arrive home. She's heard about the film because everyone is talking about it, she says. She suggests that I should use my newly minted celebrity to pressure the local mayor into giving us electricity. She says the state electricity company, Gesa, won't speak to her; they don't want to know about a project as small as ours, so the local council, the Ayuntamiento, is our only hope.

I sigh. The thought of wading into local politics over electricity is too depressing. I knew I'd get landed with the job. 'I promise I'll try,' I hear myself saying, 'on one condition: that you help me free Kendi.'

Lauren's face tightens as she mutters something about how

there is absolutely nothing she can think of which will get the dog out of the shed. It's impossible, she declares, and even more so now because she's also noticed that when the old man is out talking to his neighbours, Kendi, who used to be allowed off the chain to romp around with him, is never to be seen. She seems to be shut up the whole time. Something has happened, she solemnly intones. I am having none of it. Surely we can get a dog off a chain. This isn't Colditz. 'What I want you to do,' I say, 'is to ask Nico if I can take Kendi for a walk. You, after all, have known him for many years. Or, here's a better suggestion, why don't you bring him up here and I will ask him?'

Lauren frowns. 'I suppose I might be able to persuade Nico to come up and see you, but I don't hold out any hope he'll agree.'

And with that, she takes her leave.

It's too hot to venture outdoors, and normally I'd shutter up to contain the coolness of the old stone walls but there's an enticing breeze from the north and it seems a shame not to open the windows to the mountain air. Hundreds of years ago, those who built this house from rocks and boulders formed window openings perfectly placed to let in both the low winter sun and keep out the high rays of summer. Walking barefoot on the cold clay-tiled floors when the ground outside throbs in the heat is a real pleasure. For the rest of the day, I take it easy, reading and taking updates on the phone on the crew's progress in Palma, filming the Royals as they inspect the yachts they'll be skippering in the boat race.

For some reason, at around five in the afternoon, the heat intensifies in a last great blast before nightfall. It's only when the sun drops, at around eight, that there's a lull in temperature, enticing people out on to the streets to talk before heading indoors again, late, to eat.

———

Two young swallows siesta each afternoon, clinging to a shady ledge above my back door, silently waiting for dusk and feeding time. They've just taken wing with a lot of chirping when Lauren arrives with Nico in her car. He's smiling and has on smart khaki pants and white shirt and although he has difficulty negotiating the steps up to my patio he is full of bonhomie. He deposits himself in a wicker chair under the vine and lights a cigarette as I make for the chilled rosado and cold beer, just happy he is here, hoping that now I may be able to get through to him and find a way to get Kendi out of the shed.

We talk about everything else at first. The village, the weather, what happened to his arm and leg after his motorcycle accident and the treatment he's now receiving. He has to go to Madrid to have more grafting operations soon, he says, to repair damage to his brain. He is being very matter of fact about it all and explains he will be taken by air ambulance from Palma to get the best medical treatment on the State. I think he is being very brave about it, but ask him, 'What is going to happen to Kendi when you go into hospital? Who will walk and feed her?'

'*Mi padre,*' he quickly confirms.

'Is it possible, do you think,' I ask carefully, 'that she might come up here and see me sometime? Perhaps I can take her for a walk, I would like a dog to accompany me.'

Nico lowers his voice and says, 'Kendi, she protect *mi casa* and *mi animales,*' emphasising '*mi*' as in 'my'.

I try a different tack. 'But how can she protect your property if she is shut up all the time? If *banditos* come she can't get at them, can she?'

Nico looks uncomfortable. I know I'm touching his macho pride, which unsettles him, in common with many Spanish men I've met in recent months. I try one last shot. 'Well, can she come and protect me and my house when I'm here?'

Nico is taken aback. 'I will have to speak with *mi padre,*' he eventually demurs.

Lauren takes this as her cue to leave and suggests I give Nico a lift back to the village but he's not ready to shift just yet. He'd like another beer. He hadn't realised until now his dog is desirable.

Lauren tries to steer me away. 'It's no use pursuing it,' she says quietly as Nico nips off the end of his cigarette, 'you'll only antagonise him.'

Nico takes a long drag and begins to talk about his mother and how lost he was when she died unexpectedly while he was so ill and needed her. The night falls silent. Only when baby almond rats begin to play, galloping round the iron canopy above our heads, chasing each other with manic squeaks in and out of the vine leaves, does Nico finally move to go.

As he carefully places his walking stick in the space between the front seats and eases himself into the car, I decide I won't say anything more about Kendi tonight, but as we bump down the road and pull into the village square he turns to me and says, very seriously, he's been thinking that it's 'maybe good' Kendi comes to protect my house. We can share her. He promises to speak to his father and will tell me his decision '*mañana*'. And kisses me on both cheeks.

———

Dawn is grey in summer, oddly dark before sunrise, so for a moment the day ahead looks negotiable, as if it might not be sunny after all. This morning, however, I have no time to ponder the weather. We're sailing on the *Fortuna* again and I need shorts, T-shirts, sun cream and a swimsuit as the trip will last all day. On board will be the King's family, his daughters, son Felipe and Queen Sofia, along with their three Greek cousins, Princes Paulo and Nikolaos and Princess Alexia. I am hoping to talk to all of them but especially Prince Felipe as heir to the throne, if we can find a quiet moment.

The family are waiting for us at the Marivent where Queen Sofia has organised picnic hampers and a minibus to take us to the boat. She is immensely fond of her brother King Constantine's children who are invited each year to the Marivent for their holidays, both sets of young royals being around the same age with similar interests. None of them hang around for long. They're on the boat and ready to go, like a pack of puppies, looking forward to finding the right place to drop anchor and spend an afternoon swimming. Their favourite spot is amidst the sea turtles and dolphins just off the unspoiled island of Cabrera, where rubbish floating on the water off Mallorca is not so much in evidence. Polythene bags cause dreadful damage, particularly to turtles who swallow and choke on them.

An old couple in a small wooden Mallorquín boat, a llhaut, are fishing for shrimp, he's got on a straw hat and is burned brown. His wife, in a large brimmed hat and a black dress with an apron, is reading a newspaper under canvas stretched between two crooked masts, as the glamorous *Fortuna* slows to pass. The King is the first to wave, leaning out to greet them. The old man at the tiller lifts his hat and shouts a hearty '*bon día*' as though he's known Juan Carlos all his life, while his wife waves her rolled-up newspaper. Soon we find the perfect spot to swim and talk on camera about Mallorca and what it means to the family. Queen Sofia is sanguine about the way the island is altering. She says that although the coast is developed, in the interior the place is 'as it always has been'. There is still an agricultural way of life, whose discernible rhythm, its customs and fiestas, are still in tune with an older Mallorca. Nothing has changed, she assures me.

I can detect, while she is talking, the young Greeks getting restless, desperate to beat each other into the ocean. I need to collar Felipe before he jumps in and joins them. Nikolaos is laughing as he and his older brother Paulo jostle at the edge of the boat. Both young men have had a good dose of exile, living their lives outside a country neither has ever really known. Their father, Constantine, fled Greece during an uprising before they were born and has never been allowed to return full time.

Felipe is like his mother, Queen Sofia. He has a calm, quiet centre, obviously aware that as next in line to the throne he has to get it right. His own family's exile has been only a heartbeat away. It must be a tough call to follow a charismatic father with a sure touch yet Felipe is cool and assured about the future, as we speak to one another on camera, the boat gently rocking. He is dressed casually, in shorts and T-shirt, but manages to convey his strong sense of where Spain is heading and how he feels he has a special contribution to make as its future king. Representing his country at the Olympics has meant this summer has been good for him, given him confidence in what might be expected in the years ahead. Felipe is the quintessentially handsome prince who has been linked with every eligible European princess and the daughters of most of Spain's aristocracy. He seems to take it all in his athletic stride when I ask about the difficulty of choosing the right woman to marry. 'It's not easy marrying into royalty,' he says. 'But when I find somebody I think is capable of taking on all the duties of a queen, it won't matter whether she is royal, aristocratic or a commoner. I'll know she's right when I find her.'

There's an almighty splash and lots of shouting as everyone leaps into the ocean, calling out for us to join them. I don't need prompting. The day is too beautiful, the vast aquamarine sea too tempting to waste it on working. So I'm tipped in too. And on shore, a couple of paparazzi with long lenses sneak shots which end up in glossy magazines across the Continent.

five

Antonío must love his Muscovy duck. It's bunkered down under a buttercup-yellow parasol anchored in a pile of dirt. Antonío is the local JCB contractor and has a small-holding near the village where he keeps speckled hens, a dazzling cockbird and the Muscovy, black and white with a big red beak. The duck has been waddling in and out of an old tin bath, dug into the ground and filled with water, but today the parasol has appeared and the Muscovy is sitting contentedly under it. It must be summer.

No one dare light a match or set a fire outside now. There has been no rain since May and the hills are friable. Dried grasses crackle and pine twigs snap, too easily, underfoot. It's getting to be dangerous. Even an empty glass bottle casually chucked into the undergrowth can cause a fire if the sun's rays catch it long enough. I'm being extra careful with petrol when

I top up the generator, amazed that, with so many remote fincas without electricity in the woods, there hasn't been an accident. My generator gets so hot after a couple of hours the start button sticks. I have to press it hard to make the thing stop. I feel a kind of terror welling up every time.

Someone from the council has been diligently hanging see-through plastic bags on pine branches all along the track, hoping to trap the dreaded processionary caterpillar – its official name is Thaumetopoeidae – about to hatch from its hole in the ground and mate, unleashing a thousand offspring to march in single file through the pines, devastating the forest. There's an order out for its total arrest, hence the bags, which hang like so many baubles on a Christmas tree. They're filled with a deadly hormone that attracts and ambushes the caterpillar before it can get its teeth into the trees. Unfortunately, the council workers haven't put a bag on the magnificent pine tree that overhangs my back gate, which means that's another job for me on a cooler day. I'll have to go to the Ayuntamiento in Andratx to pick one up; it'll be a shame if out of all the trees, Thaume-whatsit decides mine is the one it wants to gobble.

Bugs in trees will have to wait because the phone's ringing and suddenly tonight's Royal supper in the Port is beginning to look dodgy. My crews are on standby but I'm being told security is freaking over the amount of people already gathering on the quay a couple of hours before the Royals are due to arrive. It's now down to the King and he won't make a decision until he gets there. If it's too intrusive he says he will call it off and have a quiet dinner with the family somewhere else. Which would be disastrous for us.

It's hard to stay positive when I also have nothing to wear. No electricity means no iron and everything I grab is creased. Jake's creeping and pouncing on my bare feet just increases my irritability. A brown linen sundress is the only answer. I reckon if it were hanging there pressed it would still end up crumpled, so it will just have to do. With my notes under one arm and the cat under the other, I manage to make it to the door without stopping for the phone, shoving Jake in the bread oven on the way out.

In the port outside the Miramar a large crowd has gathered on the pavement, the arc lights are in place, the hovering film crews dressed smartly, but it doesn't look good to me. The King will have to fight his way through this lot. Juan St Juan is standing, looking sickly, with his back to the wall as his waiters scurry about, being particularly attentive to punters who have turned up to dine on what they think is going to be a quiet night out. None of Juan's customers has been told the King will be joining them so there is consternation as film crews, a band and a hundred or so locals jostle for position.

The musicians, three men and four women, have taken trouble to dress traditionally. One of the guys I recognise – the guitarist – is the black moustachioed owner from the café next door, who's kitted out in straw hat, knee-length breeches, long socks and a fuchsia sash slung raffishly under his big tummy.

The fellow with the flute is raring to go, as are the women in their long skirts and colourful aprons, lace scarves framing their eager faces. All are impeccably turned out, they must have spent hours getting ready. My heart sinks. I have agreed that if Juan Carlos thinks the music is too loud, he will give me a thumbs down and I will step in and, trying to avoid causing offence, stop them. Even so, after they've all made such an effort, I know I'll never be able to show my face in Port d'Andratx again.

Nacho has clocked the local curly-haired photographer and a couple of other paparazzi hanging around in the crowd. 'They're over near the boats,' he points, 'do you want me to get rid of them?'

I can't imagine anything I would want less than Nacho having a punch-up right now. No, there is nothing more we can do. We will have to wait and see what the King's reaction will be.

As darkness falls a long half hour later, we find out. I was beginning to think I couldn't take the tension a moment longer when a surge of security men with walkie-talkies descend, pushing the crowd aside, clearing a way for the imminent arrival of the Royals. As the gleaming black cars pull into the port the camera lights go on and the crews move to follow the family to their table. Juan Carlos is the first out. He doesn't look pleased. His son and daughters along with the young Greek royals come next. I can see there's a discernible hesitation, a fear that it's not going to happen, they're not going to sit down to eat as exhibits in a zoo. Then Juan Carlos says something to Queen Sofia and, instead of leaving, smiles broadly, strides towards Juan St Juan, shakes him by the hand and turns and waves to the onlookers who clap and whistle back. He is going to stay and eat after all.

As the musicians begin to play and platters of fish and salad arrive in relays to their table I can sense the family relaxing, soon they're laughing and talking animatedly. After half an hour we've got all the pictures we need, the lights are dimmed but the band is still blasting it out and have another six songs to sing. I look across the tables and catch the King's eye. Mimicking a thumbs up or thumbs down, I dread his reply. Juan Carlos pushes his napkin aside and like a Roman Emperor delivers his verdict. Both thumbs, up.

This vibrant scene on a warm summer's night will later be broadcast in Germany and spark a transformation of the port. A surge of upmarket developments in this once quiet backwater will deliver huge wealth to local people in their rapid and enthusiastic embracing of a North European way of life where pricey boutiques, five-star restaurants and multi-million-dollar homes and boats drop like stardust. Soon their small port will become another St Tropez, thanks to the King choosing to dine here.

After the success of the night the crew partied. They'd received an impromptu invitation from some English women who had been dining in the Miramar and asked them back to their villa. Next morning it is hard to get the guys to focus, as they are so full of the amazing sea views and the great night they'd all had swimming in the infinity pool and dancing under the stars. Only Nacho is tetchy, again pressing me to ask the King if he would speak in Spanish on camera before we left the island. Trying not to be tetchy in return, I assure him I will.

At the Miramar the evening before I had persuaded one of the waiters to give me the juicy remains of a big piece of cod I noticed a customer, too busy staring at the Royals, hadn't eaten. It seemed a pity to waste it when the cats in the village are desperate. So a parcel, full of fishy titbits neatly wrapped in brown paper, was presented to me like the crown jewels, which it was as far as Jake was concerned. He gave me his mightiest purr, which earned him a morsel before I stowed the rest in the fridge for more deserving cases the next day.

I have decided the tabby cat who lives near Miguel the taxi driver is responsible for the kittens at the bottom of the road. Miguel does what he can, leaving piles of dried cat food out on the pavement, but she is feral and won't be handled. She is pretty, white with black and brown splodges, and is a constant conveyor of new-born cats, one batch following another. The males are ginger and the females, like their mother, multi-coloured; most meet awful ends. Even so, no one seems to have any interest in neutering her. The latest bunch of kittens are now half grown, scrawny and wormy and still, just about, managing to scavenge round the rubbish bins outside the village school. The aroma of my parcel from the

Miramar calls all cats and soon the cod has been demolished and they're ravenously attacking the dried cat food I've also brought along.

There is still no news from Nico on whether I can walk Kendi, but I've discovered, through the local paper, a rescue centre based in Palma which is appealing for funds. As I'm due at the Marivent later to film the last set-piece interview with the King, I'm going to make a detour so I'll know where to head if ever I need help in an emergency.

The sanctuary turns out to be a bunch of ramshackle huts in a run-down part of the city bordering a cemetery in a street called Jesus. It's at the bottom of a steep dirt track, in a dip in a valley, trapping the smell of animals on this hot afternoon. The dust rises, covering my clean pumps. As I'm on my way to the palace I've dressed up in a pale turquoise silk shirt over tight white knee-length pants but I've got this far and I can see dogs through the wire in their runs, barking. There are lots of cats too, irritable in their makeshift boxes. The place is locked but someone is inside, sweeping the kennels. He sees me, smiles, and comes over to explain there is no one here yet. They will come in a few hours at five. He is Mallorquín and middle-aged and as I leave I notice him talking and playing with the dogs.

It doesn't take long to get from the sanctuary to the Marivent, as the traffic through the centre of town, usually heavy in the mornings and evenings, has quietened on this hot summer afternoon. I'm feeling happier, if muckier, after my excursion to the dog's home; I now know where to come if I need help.

———

Local people call Palma a simple word, City, *La Ciutat*. It became, officially, Palma at the turn of the twentieth century, named after its earlier Roman name, Palmeria, the city of the victory palm, but the great protective wall built by the Romans didn't survive. It was flattened after surviving over a thousand years, demolished when the city got its new name. It is an *avinguda*, an avenue, now, carrying one of the city's fast roads, which I'm on today. Its zigzag course is the only obvious evidence of the old wall beneath. Palma is a beauty with plane trees and palms shading wide avenues, steep stone steps linking ancient thoroughfares, heritage gems at every turn. There are fragments of other historic city walls built in the centuries following Rome around every corner.

There's even a small bath house erected by the Moors a millennia ago, the Banys Arabs, which like a button in a button box lies pressed in the Old Quarter of Palma, jumbled amongst so many other glorious remains. The appeal of these baths, like so much else here, is how easy it is to imagine myself a Moor in need of peace and relaxation. I'd start with the steam bath (the calderium) before hopping into a warm one (a tepidarium) and lie there, under the vaulted roof supported by twelve stone pillars, now a thousand years old. The best bit is up aloft. Skylights in the roof allow in just enough sun to warm me below but I'm afraid, no matter how tempting, I haven't time to daydream today. I need to find somewhere quiet and contemplative to think through the vital questions I need to ask Juan Carlos as this will be my last opportunity.

So much has cropped up in the course of filming I want to be clear what's still needed to finish the project. Near the Real Club Náutico there's a car park surrounded by pink and white oleander bushes where warm sea air will help me concentrate. I haven't yet talked about the Olympics, Mallorca, or bullfighting with the King, or what I would dearly love him to address, but know he won't: the Franco years.

Mallorca suffered badly under the dictator. The island was an attack base for Franco's forces striking out against their countrymen on the mainland. There were blockades and food shortages and worse. Thousands were tortured and murdered on Mallorca as were thousands more on mainland Spain but today it's only old men in bars who dare pass on the whispered secrets. 'The killing fields,' they say of Santa Ponsa, a holiday resort in the south-west of the island. Could that really be true? In the 1970s politicians from all parties signed up to *omertà* – silence – there would be no witch-hunt. No one would be held accountable for what happened during and after the civil war. But life, memories and hatred don't always conform to good intent. Franco is in the past, and I will have to do as I agreed and not task Juan Carlos to recollect the man who made him King.

From my car I can see and hear young men who have arrived from all over Europe for the big yacht race. Most, of course, don't give a fig about Franco. There's a buzz in the making ready of fast boats for action, last-minute checks on equipment, ropes and tackle for the Copa del Rey. Juan Carlos will skipper the midnight-blue *Bribon*, gleaming on the quayside.

Towards the end of a long filming session there comes a time when the crew get a sense of whether the movie is going to work or not and behave accordingly. By the time I reach the Marivent the cameras have been rigged, the cream leather sofa for the interview positioned and cables for lights woven round every table and ornate chair. The crew are in an exuberant mood, not helped by some odd, colourful bonnets that have appeared and are being passed around, tried on and taken off, by the Royal family. Somehow in this air of end-of-term recklessness I have to concentrate on finishing the film. We sit down, Juan Carlos and I, side by side on the sofa, with the ocean glittering behind us, and talk about achievement, pride and heritage. Juan Carlos tackles bullfighting by comparing it with fox hunting in the UK. Your country chases foxes, there's no difference, he opines. At least the fox has a chance to escape, I rally, but he is, of course, not about to enter into argument. His political antennae are too keen. As a Spanish male monarch his role is to fervently support the insupportable, or at least to be seen to.

Our talk ends on a high with Juan Carlos acknowledging his remarkable year and how Spain faces a dynamic, gilded future – then Nacho moves in. As Paloma unclips Juan Carlos's microphone, I manage to head off Nacho, telling him under no circumstances is this film going to be spoiled by asking for an interview that was never on the agenda from the outset and certainly is not on now. He looks murderous. Paloma steps in to lighten the moment. She's brought a camera, she says, and isn't going to leave until someone takes a picture of her with 'her' king. She then gives Juan Carlos her best toothy smile and brazenly suggests he sit next to her on the sofa. Juan Carlos demurely does as he is told, but Paloma, wanting the full works, snuggles closer, then a touch more, until he finally gives in, conceding defeat with a big grin and a royal bear hug.

This snapshot is the last. After Nacho informs his bosses that there will be no King speaking Spanish, in a grand Latino flourish they pull out of the deal and order the crew home. I'm sorry to see them depart and a bit perplexed at the strop but I've got what I want: the film is complete. It will now be down to Grampian in Scotland to parley with the Spaniards in Madrid over how much money they'll get back.

It is an anti-climax in so many other ways as well. I've spent the year in a bubble pressed against privilege, wealth and glamour, one minute filming delicious buildings of great age in a hidden Spain, the next pitched into the dynamic of a nation's coming-of-age party. Now I am back at my unfinished house in the unlit hills wrapping up the memory. The warm calm of the valley is beyond welcome after the filming but it takes a while to come to terms with what I've seen and the way things actually are.

Across Spain, Europe's money is deluging new roads, bridges, tunnels. Whole cities are being re-developed with the aim of social equality. Human rights are prerequisite but Europe's attitude towards animals is, to say the least, arbitrary. The EC could have insisted its new members adopt a statutory animal welfare programme before any cash got handed out. It would have saved a ton of grief. As it is, Mallorca, soon to be one of the wealthiest islands in the world, gives precious little to the creatures in its midst and, as I will discover in the years ahead, fights bitterly anyone who dares attempt it.

I had planned to spend the rest of the summer relaxing in the Mediterranean before returning to the UK to cut the Juan Carlos film but with no electric light and no prospect of getting any, with Kendi out of sight and no sound from Nico, I am beginning to get edgy.

————

It was the start button, stuck, that did it. The generator had been running for a couple of hours and I could sense something was wrong because the thing was steaming. When I reached in to shut it down, the button jammed again. On and on it groaned and revved. I knew I had to find a way to stop fuel getting to the engine but was terrified I'd pull out the wrong piece of kit and cause an explosion. It was the middle of a hot afternoon, siesta time, with no one around. The engine droned on.

I decided the best solution was to turn my back and leave it until it ran out of fuel, but the machine wasn't having any of it. Half an hour later, smoke billowed out. If the generator caught fire the whole valley would go up in these dry conditions. Me too. I ran into the kitchen, soaked a towel and rushed back. To get at the petrol supply I had to prise open the hot metal cover juddering over the engine. As the lid clanked to the floor the revs thickened but I could just make out a tiny lever under the tank. I reached in and pressed. In a second or two there was a cough. Then another. Finally and unbelievably the machine croaked.

How did Joe know? The phone rang just as the generator came out with its hands up. He laughed when I told him of my panic in the heat. It would be something simple, he said. He'd be able to see to it. Could I manage without power until he could fix a flight? Could I? I'd haul buckets of water out of the *cisterna* till eternity if it meant I never had to use the generator again.

With Joe and his boys on the way Jake and I had to fix the beds, dig out some mosquito nets and check for creepy-crawlies. A pink setting sun was sugar-coating a few fluffy clouds by the time I had shooed off the gecko lurking incognito on the window ledge and plumped up the beds. Clouds in a summer Mediterranean sky mean change is on the way. Jake closed his eyes, rolled over on the pressed linen sheet with his paws above his head and purred.

———

Sancho has sent a message: there are some strange men in his bar asking questions about me. He thinks they are paparazzi and ordered them out. They want to know where my house is and he certainly isn't about to tell them.

The Spanish newspapers have seen a blonde on the *Fortuna* and are after me. I've always laid low in August, a dangerous month for anyone in the public eye who wants privacy. With everyone on holiday the paparazzi decamp too. Some relish the experience more than others although it's hard to avoid photographers if you have a glossy home on a honeypot island. Michael Douglas and his Mallorquín wife Diandra are a hot ticket in their cliff-top retreat in the north near Deia. Their restoration of the romantic home of Archduke Salvatore, who fell in love with the island over a hundred years ago, is now a summer pit stop for Hollywood stars such as Jack Nicholson and Warren Beatty, who seem happy to pump up the action for photographers, intoxicated as they all are with fun in the European sun.

Deia is quite a hike from me. Built against a steep mountainside, it is a village of enchanting stone homes reached by a precipitous road wound tight round the west coast. Deia was made famous by the poet Robert Graves, who was encouraged to come to Mallorca by his friend and mentor Gertrude Stein in the 1930s. 'So you suggest Mallorca as a place to settle down?' he asked her. 'Yes,' she replied, 'it's paradise – if you can stand it.'

When I first arrived on the island, Robert Graves' widow Beryl still lived in their low modern house on the edge of Deia. I remember she had a thing about Earl Grey tea, which I once dropped off for her when Deia was having a late-afternoon snooze. I walked half a mile to the tiny cobbled bay below her house, down the steep road Robert Graves built so he might bathe more easily in the ocean. Deia I thought a bit overwhelming with its vertiginous mountainscape of trees and rock. A little too closed in for my taste.

At my end of the gentler Sierra Tramuntana ridge, Joe and his sons, seven-year-old Jack and nine-year-old Ben, have come out in big red blobs from mosquito bites. They've decided the nets I've rigged from a hook in an old beam above their beds are like frilly skirts 'cissies' wear, so they tied them up like wigwams, leaving them wide open to night bites. Every bit of them, it seems, has been munched but it doesn't deter them. They've come on an adventure their mates would die for, they say. Within a day they've hired mountain bikes and set off, coated in factor 50, along the pine-needled path on to the high range. They've dumped their rucksacks and left me to get on with taking care of business. Which means food. I've hit on lighting a charcoal fire in the old bread oven and cooking supper in what is in effect a little cave. It means kicking out the almond rats and spiders but once the fire gets going it stays hot for hours, a novelty which keeps everyone interested and amused.

Amid the day's snorkelling and bicycling their father trails oily nuts and bolts from the cannibalsed generator and manages to find a small second-hand, friendly looking substitute from a local builder as a back-up. It will soon become my mainstay, because, with the red genny still lying in bits, Joe succumbs after a week to some particularly venal bugs. It's his own fault. I don't know what kind of beasts have done the damage, but I reckon he's picked them up in the long grass walking in his shorts through the sheep fields higher up the valley. From his ankles to his thighs, purple weals have begun to ooze and the antiseptic cream I've got from the *farmacia* in Andratx is unfortunately not working. On the morning his legs turn septic I spot the glint of a camera lens in a pine tree on the hill.

I had opened the shutters to let in the morning light. In August, the sun takes its time to stride the high pines on the eastern hill before shafting strong, intermittent rays across the valley. It was one of these early, searching rays that caught the camera hidden in a tree on the opposite side. I have developed an instinct for lenses of the long-range persuasion but this time, when I glanced again, I thought I saw a hammock too. It was unbelievable. A hammock was definitely strung between two pine trees; whoever was in it must have been up there all night. I quickly closed the window. If there was one photographer out there, there'd be more and I had no intention of letting any of them steal pictures of me. What I wanted to know was were they all perched up pine trees? And if so, I hope the poisonous caterpillars had marched in and got each and every one of them on the way down.

When I tumble downstairs to tell everyone we are surrounded, Joe is screwed up at the breakfast table in pain.

His legs, he moans, are on fire. Ben and Jack, agog with the drama of grown men climbing trees to stake out their quarry, want the low-down. How high up are they? Can they go and look? Joe decides he's had enough. He's going home on the first plane out, otherwise he'll end up in hospital. And, under no circumstances, he growls as he crawls up the stairs to pack, is he going to be seen hobbling to a car with me in front of the world's press. He doesn't want his picture in the papers. No thanks. He doesn't know who might see it. It could lead to all kinds of trouble. And would I phone for a taxi?

As the boys shuffle off to gather their belongings, I beg the man who runs the local taxi to come up the hill to collect them. If you drive very slowly, I implore, you won't damage your car – at all – on the rocks. Eventually he relents saying he's already heard there are plenty of nasty people up my road. Am I going to be all right? I tell him, *gracias*, I will be.

Once Joe and the boys have gone I phone Boris. Can he come up and check out the place? I'm not sure what my next move should be. Should I try and leave or stay? It isn't fun being spied on. I'm not sure how many photographers are hanging around and what they'll do if I make an appearance. Having a black lens the size of a dinner plate pointed at you from the bushes is a bit like being kicked in the stomach. And I, of course, am not the kind of person to take this calmly. How dare they come here and do this to me in my un-glam place, which I have deliberately chosen miles away from their usual glitzy haunts?

Through the slats in the shutters I can see Boris bouncing up the road, reversing his car right up against the back door. He's brought Bruce. Both are wearing large, khaki, wide-brimmed hats with toggles under their chin, to hide their faces, they say. Why, like Joe, they should want to disguise themselves is odd but I am grateful to have their practical if rather self-regarding support. They tell me Gunther had woken from his slumbers and counted six Spanish photographers and reporters lurking in the valley, so they've cleared the back of the car for me to get away without anyone knowing, adding that Gunther is now on guard, fully charged to counter any fresh invasion. He will, they tell me, keep an eye on the place.

After all this, I feel I can't very well let them down, so I scramble into the boot hoping no one will spot me. Bumping down the road, curled up under a blanket, I miss what happens next but suddenly from further up the hill a massive boulder comes rolling down, crashing against Boris's car before settling on the road in front. Two hefty men jump out of the bushes but Boris is quicker. 'Oh, shit,' he mutters as he dodges round the rock and speeds away, with me jolting up and down in the back.

I suppose, in retrospect, it was wrong to attempt evasion. Soon word spread that things were turning nasty. The encounter with the boulder had been relayed round the village and posses of folk were being despatched to investigate and report back.

Later, someone confirms the paparazzi have gone, they've been seen driving out of the village so it is, I am assured, all clear for me to return. I don't need much of an excuse, and in any case, Jake needs feeding and I am sick of the disruption.

I walk right into it, of course, or more precisely, into Gunther, who is in the middle of the track in khaki fatigues getting agitated. He has a red and white bandanna round his blond curls and a pair of tightly laced army boots up to his kneecaps. A white car with a man and woman is lurching slowly towards him. Gunther's got his hand up, like a policeman, calling them to stop, but the guy in the car has a camera and is reeling off frame after frame of an angry Gunther, now bawling something unmentionable in Spanish. What takes place next happens as if in slow motion: the guy with the camera is laughing, the next moment he's bellowing as Gunther grabs a huge rock from the side of the road, hoists it above his head and lobs it with a wonderful force straight at the car. I shut my eyes as the rock leaves Gunther's grip. When I look again, the car is in fast reverse, its windscreen shattered, the boulder wedged like an unwelcome passenger between the car's two front seats. It had been close.

Later that night, I'm getting ready for bed and hear something rustling in the field outside. There's a full moon. Creeping to the window, opening it ever so carefully, through the crack in the shutters I can just make out Gunther's bandanna crawling through the undergrowth. 'Gunther?' I call in a loud whisper.

Back from out of the grass comes 'Shhh…'

'What are you doing?'

'I'm patrolling,' he growls.

'Gunther, come here.' Gunther springs up glancing right and left.

'I have had a good idea,' he calls up to my bedroom window.

'What?'

'I vill hoot like an owl to let you know it's me. Too vit too vit,' he demonstrates, 'and you will respond so that I know it's you' – and at this he cups his hands to his mouth and warbles – 'Too voo too voo.'

'But Gunther,' I try reasoning, 'wouldn't it be more straightforward if I simply asked, "Is that *you*, Gunther?" And you can say, "Yes it is."'

———

The next day, after all the excitement, nothing of any consequence appears in the Spanish press except a grainy black-and-white photo taken of me in shorts and sandals striding down the road. A female reporter notes that for my age it's surprising I haven't any cellulite.

Now that the press have discovered me, however, they begin to stake me out. After a particularly bad bout of fast car chases down one-way streets and the desperate ploy of taking someone else's plane ticket to get back to the UK quickly I began to think Gunther's 'Too wit Too woo' was not so daft after all.

six

I adore getting hot, so hot the only way to cool off is to roll into the ocean from a pebbled beach and swim. Most mornings I'll walk through the woods with towels, a bottle of water, goggles and a book and reach the coast by nine, my skin nicely toasted. Swimming with the sun on my back out to a headland and round into the next bay is always a joy, even though an occasional troublesome jellyfish crawls alongside me too. Jellyfish usually turn up in their thousands early in the season, pulsating their purple tentacles in the tide, but with a bit of encouragement and an offshore wind, they soon buzz off. For a creature so small they do a deal of damage. I carry a tube of anti-jellyfish cream in case I'm stung. Others swear by urine and all sorts of other contortionist remedies, none easy to administer on a crowded public beach and definitely not an option if, like me, you're concerned about being caught out on camera.

A House in the High Hills

Today, in late August, nothing can disrupt a swim in an ocean this still. The clarity of the water is incredible, shoals of little fish hoover up near the surface and lower down, above patches of golden sand between rocks, larger, more colourful fish investigate.

I've got to know, now, those who come at the same time of day to this spot to swim. They are charming, mainly German, most of whom live in the village. I imagine they once were teachers because they read weighty books, take an interest in politics and speak beautiful English. They are all great friends, changing uninhibitedly in front of one another for their long-distance swim each day. This morning there's much fulminating about corruption in Andratx. Illegal building is beginning to blight the area and they're discussing the backhanders officials are given as though it's accepted legal practice. 'But of course it happens,' they lecture at my naivety. 'Everyone's into bribery here. There's so much black-market money coming in, especially from Germany, the place is awash in cash. The local mayor is the main culprit, along with his planning officer. You'll see.'

A dusty beat-up old car has arrived with a couple who come each morning from a finca high in the hills. She has red hair and stands as a dancer might. Her partner is an artist with a magnificent moustache. Everyone greets them warmly and talk about dirty dealings in the council are put aside. There are no jellyfish today, someone solemnly declares. I notice they are all very supple and don't stay long in the sun after they've snorkelled round the bay.

In any case it's Wednesday and market day in Andratx so everyone packs up early to join the scrum of local women who muscle with their bags on wheels to be first at the fruit and veg stalls. If you don't hasten, you queue, which is no fun in this heat. Police straddle the main street screeching whistles at busloads of tourists. Counterfeit Gucci bags, cheap clothes, massive brassieres and knickers, cheeses, olives, pickles and pans overwhelm stalls on every side as crowds take hundreds of half-steps to negotiate the narrow alleyways. There is no hurry, it's a total waste of time, as the menfolk clustering in the corner bars have so expertly sussed.

I usually make for a stall in the centre of the melee, which sells home-made pesto, fresh basil and small sweet tomatoes grown in a local garden which are scooped up quickly by those in the know. Today I keep bumping into the boys who inhabit the bars in the village, here to find cheap trousers for their building work; every able-bodied bloke it seems builds – mostly around their complicated love lives.

Rex, a Belgian, is tall, diffident and good-looking in a dishevelled sort of way. He falls in love regularly, always introducing his latest as 'my fiancée', which tickles the woman in tow but usually means it's not going to last. He tackles all kinds of building projects to raise money for a quick escape when he gets in too deep. Even so, by the time he's got the cash the woman he's about to ditch has usually given up on him and gone off with someone else. Rex is searching through a pile of polyester overalls with a fluffy pup on a lead he found scavenging round his dustbins. The pup has a bandaged paw, her claws torn trying to find food, but she's now moved in with Rex, which isn't pleasing his new fiancée.

His great mate, Mick, is with him. The two of them were once partners in their own building firm but thought better of it. Mick is currently into photography although he also fancies himself as bit of a Mallorquín Bob Dylan, soulfully belting out songs whenever there's a musical get-together. His talents and big brown eyes are much appreciated by the retinue of glamorous girlfriends he attracts. He lopes along to the stall selling sobrasada sausage.

Rex asks if I'd like a lift back to the village, he's heading in that direction and his pick-up is parked in the square. He hands me the pup on the lead while he pays for his bargain trews and I set off, squeezing my way through the crowds. His truck is loaded with Mexican terracotta cooking pots, piled up and roped together. 'What on earth, Rex?' I ask as the pup and I fall into the front seat.

'It's a great deal I've come across,' he says. 'I've imported hundreds from South America to flog here as barbecues. I'm going to end up loaded.'

The pup settles softly on my lap, her poor paw resting on my knees as Rex crunches through the gears. We have only gone about fifty yards when there's a great splintering crash. A pot has deposited itself on the road behind us. It's bust in two. Rex swears and jumps out, calling me to help. As hooting cars pile up, he grabs the biggest of the lumps while I scramble with the entangled pup to retrieve what's left. Rex is smirking as we flee the scene. 'Will you marry me?' he wants to know.

The tiny restaurant in the village, where Emmy Lou once helped with the cooking, has been taken over by Rodriquez, a young Catalan. Inside it's painted the colours of the sun, earth and sky. There are clay tiles on the floor, white walls and cobalt blue and yellows on every pillar and arch. It is very relaxed and the food delicious but Rodriquez's great and marvellous skill is his guitar playing. At night, after hanging up his apron, he brings out a stool and blows the place away. He plays from the heart, his fingers finding chords without a musical score. Today he's fixing the menu on the door, laughing with Nico who shouts over to me, 'See you in Sancho's, Selina.'

Just now, Nico is not drinking alcohol. His doctor has told him it is not good for his condition. He orders a lacao instead, a sickly looking milk drink laced with chocolate in a small glass bottle. I detect a contrived seriousness and wonder what Nico's up to. Purposefully he props his stick against the chair and leans towards me, tipping his head ever so slightly back just like his father, and sucks in his breath, sharply. 'Plenty problems in your *casa*, eh?' I try a smile, not sure where this is leading. 'Plenty men,' his eyes widen, '*aqui*.'

'Here?'

Nico nods knowingly. And then I've got it. I haven't seen Nico since the press fiasco. 'Oh, that. It's all okay now,' I assure him.

But Nico is not responding the way he normally does. He purses his lips and shakes his head slowly. What else is he going to offer up, I wonder. And then suddenly and quietly, he says, 'You need a dog to patrol your *casa*.'

Is he saying what I think he's saying? I am trying so hard not to leap ahead of what I believe is coming next, holding myself back, waiting for Nico to declare his hand. And then, like a gambler with his winning ticket, he slowly reaches into his pocket and plonks, smack on the table, a set of keys. 'These are for you,' he says. They are the keys to the kennel. 'Kendi can come and protect you whenever you want.'

I want to hug him. After weeks of anguish I've been let out of gaol. 'Does your father agree?'

'*Sí, sí*, you are a woman who needs help.' Nico is now at his most macho.

'Can I go and let her out this minute?'

'*Sí*, I come with you.'

The walk up the road to Kendi is interminable. Nico is relishing his new role as he enunciates every syllable ve-ry slowly, milking his new-found importance while my mind clutters with how this arrangement is actually going to work and whether he really means it.

A plastic bag of stale bread left for the hens and goats is hooked on the gates as Nico fumbles with the lock. A bantam runs out, squawking, ducking under the grape vine to join its friends in the chicken run. There's a door in the shed at the far end which has no window and is also locked. Nico fiddles with the keys again until it opens, and steps back to allow me to enter ahead of him. Inside, it is putrid; a rope hanging from the rafters catches my hair and cobwebs stick to my cheek.

Nico calls her name. Kendi. She makes a small squeaking sound in recognition but can't move towards us because she's tied to the wall with a chain. Nico is soon there, patting her on the head, she licking and fussing him as though he's done nothing wrong. Her tail thumps heavily on the earth floor as I am formally introduced. 'Can I take her with me now?' I say, desperate to get her out of this claustrophobic hole.

'Of course,' Nico says as he unclips the chain.

Kendi is still on her best behaviour, waiting for her owner to decide what's to happen next. Once she's told what she can do, she follows Nico as he makes for the door. Outside, Nico reaches for a lead and solemnly hands it to me. It all seems too simple. Kendi has her ears on alert, looking in anticipation at the lead. Let's go.

She really is a lovely dog, trotting up the road close to heel, glancing up at me for my approval. There's no pulling or tugging. She's been trained to walk with Nico, obviously. But when we get to the house, well, it's pathetic. The moment she's off the lead she runs and runs before collapsing, panting, on the steps up to the patio.

Her coat is not in good condition either. It's rough and dandruffy but I'm so happy she's here. I wonder how long she will be able to stay.

A little later a thunderstorm strafes the sky. For some

reason the island magnifies the sound and passion of the elements. A blackness comes first, then an obliteration with a few drops of rain. The early rain has a beat as it hits the tiles, but soon, with the deluge, it morphs into what sounds like a fervent, clapping crowd. Kendi is terrified. She shivers and presses against me trying to find somewhere she can hide. I missed the lightning but smelled it when it struck. Sulphur before the crack. The pink blowsy blossom on the trumpet vine plops sodden to the ground as water cascades off the roof down the pipe into the *cisterna*. Valuable and appreciated stuff, but delivered with such drama it smarts.

After the closeness comes the airiness as the storm passes and the temperature drops. Out of the hedge flaps the hoopoes, now a family of four, coursing the newly soaked earth for insects. Their long, pointed, dun-coloured neck feathers mirror their sharp, probing beaks, so they resemble a purposeful gang of double-headed hammers going about their business. A slight movement and they're gone, undulating back to the bushes, weaving and leaving a flash of black and white zebra striping behind.

Carter, Emmy Lou's son, is not as bashful as the birds. He's got his sights on the old plum tree and has called in to ask if I'll let him give the tree a 'hair cut' when I leave. He's been reading all about pruning, he says, and insists it will improve fruiting. I know he sneaked in early in the year to pick the plums when I wasn't around but Kendi is welcoming him with such big licks I say, well, all right then. He grudgingly enquires how I managed to get her out of the compound as he can see how settled she is already and how good-natured but he's on his way to the village for a fiesta and doesn't want to hang around. I would like to have asked if he might take Kendi with him, so he can put her back in her shed as I'm dreading doing it. She has had a good run and a little dog meat from a can I found in the pantry, just enough not to upset her tummy, but I can see he's not interested so Kendi and I make the journey by ourselves, she meekly allowing me to tie her back up to the wall in her shed and do what I have to, filling her bowl with fresh water from a tap outside, telling her I'll see her early tomorrow. Trying to be positive.

————

It's a good time of year to get to know Kendi. It's cooler now and soon the 'second spring' will come when the seeds that have lain dormant through the hot summer sprout and shoot up with the rain. Everything in the valley will turn a fresh bright green but first there is a harvest to reap. The pomegranates, fat and rosy, are about to tear and fall. Figs turn from green to ripe black almost overnight. It's also almond picking time. The soft shells of the almonds, like the pomegranates, have split and will soon spill hard kernels on the ground. I shake off the cobwebs covering the roll of green net in the shed, unfurl it around the trees like a carpet and tickle the almonds with a long cane to encourage them to tumble into it obligingly.

A House in the High Hills

I've set aside the next few days to try and pick as much fruit as possible but the morning I set off to pick up Kendi again a white, gauzy blob has suddenly appeared, swinging from a branch of the pine tree at my back gate. I know exactly what it is. The dreaded processionary caterpillar has arrived and woven its nest on my lovely tree. Soon zillions of them will be on the march, which means if I don't take immediate action, the tree will die. I can see they have already chewed their way along one large branch so if I can saw it off along with the nest, I may be in with a chance.

First though: Kendi. I have a bit of a struggle with the lock on her door but suddenly it gives, the key turns and I'm in, the sun penetrating the gloom where sacks of corn for chickens and beans are stacked along with old farm implements and buckets of eggs. Gruesome-looking muzzles and goat bells on leather collars hang from nails hammered into the wall. Kendi is quivering, excited to see me, but as I go to untie her, something scurries over my sandalled foot. When I look again, it's a rat, a proper rat. Horrified, I see they're everywhere.

The moment we're back at the house I'm in the right frame of mind to vent my wrath on the caterpillars. Kendi doesn't know what to make of me shinning up the pine tree dressed in shorts and T-shirt and armed with a handsaw. She's sitting on her haunches, ears corkscrewed, waiting as I attack the branch, my back wedged against the trunk, trying hard not to do myself a mischief. The soft resinous wood soon cracks, taking the nest and branch crashing to the ground with all the caterpillars on board. Instantly I feel better.

As I drag the debris to the middle of the field Kendi follows at a distance. She's obviously had experience of this kind of thing and is not going to get too close. I can see by her expression that she never thought this was a good idea in the first place. And soon I realise why. I start to burn. A painful, itchy sensation quickly creeps along the skin on my legs, arms and hands. Scratching makes it worse. I turn red and feel as if I'm on fire. The secretions by the caterpillars covering the bark of the branch have done for me. It will be a week before the prickling stops and my skin clears up, enough time to learn another painful lesson about life in Mallorca. Of all the creatures on the planet, only the resident hoopoe bird is equipped to handle the processionary caterpillar. If you ask me, hoopoes must have throats like battle-ships.

It wasn't long before I came to the conclusion that my encounter with the caterpillars pretty much summed up the way the island behaved. Only those hefted to the place, who'd been here for years, were able to clean up.

Which meant, if I was going to hoover up poisonous creepy-crawlies intent on making life difficult for me, I'd have to be as sharp – if not sharper – than any marauding bird. At least that's the way I felt when I first went into bat with Lauren for an electricity supply soon after my encounter with the paparazzi.

Lauren had fixed a meeting with the local planning department at the town hall because she'd lost impetus getting folk to sign up for her electricity project.

As I'd already spent a day with her, queueing and form-filling in the bronze-tinted edifice of Gesa HQ in Palma and had got nowhere, I couldn't see how we'd fare any better with another bunch of officials closer to home, but Lauren was insistent. If we could get them to see our plight, they could lean on Gesa to give us electricity 'if only for social reasons', she said, whatever that meant.

When we arrived for our meeting, held in a poky room opposite a bar in an Andratx backstreet, some men in suits greeted us politely, assuring us they would do what they could, agreeing that it was indeed absurd that in the late twentieth century some homes in Mallorca still didn't have a vital supply of power but could they suggest we go away, put together a project signed by all those who want electricity and come back to them?

We were back to the beginning again, but not for long. A few carefully dropped hints from well-meaning locals later and I began to get the message.

It was only when I was officially informed by the planners many months later I would need special permission to have electricity and would have to tunnel through rock and dig up the road all the way from the village to my house so that the cable would be underground at least a metre deep, all of which would cost thousands, that I began to understand the true measure of my predicament. I was one of those caterpillars who had just built a nest and along had come a hoopoe and gobbled me up.

Turned out, I wasn't the only one. Once Boris Becker arrived in the east of the island and Claudia Schiffer had become ensconced in the south the German market rapidly became hooked on wild Mallorca. Like the caterpillars, they processed to the island in their thousands. The Brits soon followed: Richard Branson invested in a hotel in Deia; Andrew Lloyd Webber, Annie Lennox and Catherine Zeta Jones ended up in historic houses along the north-west coast, and with such profile came wealth.

A sticky trail of dodgy money, mainly from Germany, soon led all the way to the Med. German deutschmarks slewed into Spanish property just before the euro went universal. Better the marks from under the bed be put into bricks and mortar than converted into an untried coinage. The Spanish were only too eager to assist. A new Spanish phrase came into currency. If you wanted something built were you going to pay in black or white money? The average weekly Spanish wage remained well below the European norm but no one officially admitted it was low because most of it was black. Black money could be spent in supermarkets, white kept the accountants happy.

Politicians salivating at the prospect of an invasion that showed no sign of abating began to put a price on tranquillity, belatedly realising that solitude is something islands are supposed to have in their DNA. Mallorca had tons of it. Old ruins, long deserted because they were cut off and unman-ageable, were now not only desirable but valuable.

My house went from being an interesting old finca in the Sierra Tramuntana, to a protected Grade 1 property. It got an upgraded name, '*rustico protegido*' and a new classification. My house got drafted under an environment law to some-thing called a Terreno ANEI without anyone bothering to tell me. It was all done ostensibly for good environmental reasons but with political control came power.

It wasn't long before the pressure of mountains of inter-national money brought greed and a brazen manipulation of planning laws so that when developers wanted to build, they handed over a bung. Lawyers for each side left the room while the deed was done. I missed out on all the ribaldry because I bought my property before the rush but it didn't mean I avoided the clunking fist when it fell.

It descended soon after Lauren casually announced I was now in charge of her electricity project as she had got a new job in the north of Spain and would be leaving the island, temporarily. 'I'll be back,' she threatened, 'and with luck you might have the valley lit up by then.'

We had just had our meeting in Andratx and were supposed to be rustling up signatures from our neighbours. Coming after the water drilling fiasco, I wasn't happy and told her so. Under no circumstances was I going to waste any more time trudging to Gesa in Palma or the Ayuntamiento in

above: Co-anchors Frank Bough and Nick Ross along with astrologer Russell Grant and me on the red sofa. We presented the UK's first breakfast TV show which aired in January 1983.

right: With Jeff Banks promoting *The Clothes Show* in 1986.

left: First glimpse of the ruin in the high Tramuntana hills of south-west Mallorca.

below: The patio, an oasis of colour in the warmth of a spring day in that first year of my finding the house.

below: My garden of olive and almond trees in high summer, the pink of the trumpet vine smothering the pergola, an almighty buzz of bees busy amidst its blossom.

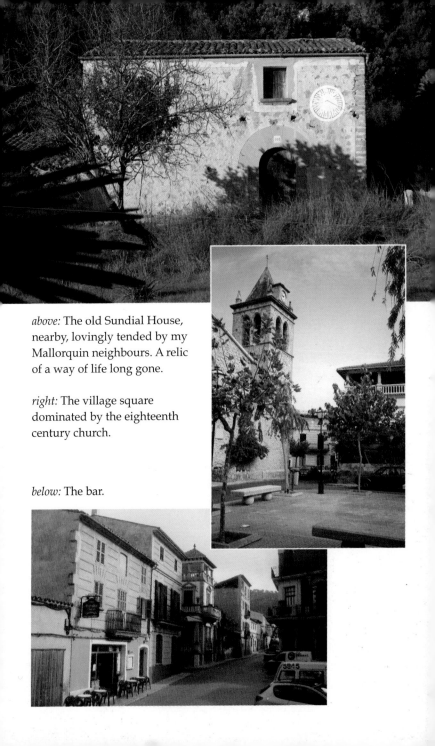

above: The old Sundial House, nearby, lovingly tended by my Mallorquin neighbours. A relic of a way of life long gone.

right: The village square dominated by the eighteenth century church.

below: The bar.

above: The village in the valley,
seen from the hill beside my house.

below: The beautiful beach at San Telm
looking towards the island of Dragonera.

right: Working on the script for the documentary 'The Year of Spain'.

below: Prince Felipe on board the *Fortuna* attempting to concentrate on questions about his future role as heir apparent to the Spanish throne.

left: King Juan Carlos in high spirits adjusting a bonnet he'd plonked on my head after we'd finished the documentary. Can't figure out, even now, where he found it.

left: Madrid and journey's end, Juan Carlos having piloted us into the remote mountains of Spain.

left: A moment of rare relaxation by the pool.

below: Kendi enjoys the sunshine.

The photos above show some of the trials and tribulations of making a swimming pool, but it was definitely worth it in the end.

© Andrew Montgomery

above: Whitewashed walls and colourful pottery inside my cool home.

below: The bare branches of the fig trees are the only hint that this is winter in Mallorca.

Andratx. If anyone wanted electricity they would have to get it themselves.

That's not how it got translated, however. Word soon got round that here was I, a newcomer, who had bought a house knowing it didn't have electricity, now demanding ugly poles and wire be erected on beautiful land for my own selfish ends. Before I realised what was happening, Gunther invited me for the first time into his home to soften me up. He was keen, he said, to show me four big ship batteries he had installed in his kitchen, rigged by cables through the roof to a solitary solar panel. He pointed to an electric light bulb hanging desultorily in his kitchen and said this was all the light he needed. That wasn't the finish of it. Outside his back door, he proudly pointed to an arch of used plastic water bottles, connected, spout to tail, each to the other, which dripped water warmed by the sun into a washing-up bowl. This was Gunther's way of heating water and I was inordinately impressed. He then took me back inside and said he didn't want electricity to come to the valley. So this was what the conducted tour was all about.

'Gunther,' I said, 'I totally understand, but I am not talented like you. I am not able to devise ingenious green solutions to the major problem this valley faces, which is the noise from diesel generators and your diesel generator in particular. It pollutes the air and kills the tranquillity of this place.' I felt myself warming mightily to my grievance. 'And what's more, what's the problem with having wooden poles carrying electric cables? They'll blend in and be hidden in the trees? I bet we won't even see them.'

At this, Gunther threw back his shoulders and spat. 'You'll see, there'll be neon lights and strip joints all the vay up the valley if electricity comes.'

'Now, Gunther,' I said soothingly, 'you know very well we won't have strip joints.'

'You vait and see,' he hissed.

The next day, I was shopping in the village when the second wave came. Francine sidled up. 'I want to speak to you,' she said menacingly. As Francine had been stony-faced for weeks I wasn't surprised she'd been delegated to diss me.

'People don't like you,' she began, launching into a peculiar little war dance. 'Why don't you sell up and go? You'll get plenty of money for your house, you can go and live somewhere else where you're not so big.'

I think she meant where I was not so well known, but it seemed rude to interrupt her. 'You've only been here a bit, we've been here twenty-five years, you bought your house knowing you didn't have electricity, how dare you now try to bring it to the valley when we don't want it?'

I didn't think now was the time or the place to remind her that she was being hypocritical, driving as she did to the port each day to use a friend's electricity to wash and iron her clothes. No, that was too petty on a busy village street. 'Are you leaving?' she demanded.

'No.'

'You should.'

As I'd had a master class in cattiness from women who were experts in the field, the so-called 'bitches of Fleet Street', Jean Rook of the *Daily Express* and Lynda Lee Potter of the *Daily Mail*, who had regularly and gleefully dissected my every move, Francine's outburst was, to say the least, tiddly by comparison. Only when she burst forth with 'A lot of people feel great resentment towards you, you ought to be careful because you might find your house threatened. It could be burned down,' did I snap.

'That's a lynch mob mentality, Francine.'

It didn't deter her. She then delivered what she considered a blinder. Her voice quivering she said, '*Ultima Hora*,' – a local Spanish newspaper – 'says you're finished in television.'

Oh really?

'Well, Francine,' I finally said, 'tough.'

This is probably when I should have left Mallorca. My bolthole had been uncovered, along with bad feelings from my neighbours, but I wasn't the kind of person to give in. In any case who was going to look after Jake and Kendi? No one I'd come across here.

It was one of those warm late September days, of figs and fennel, when Boris re-appeared. He'd come to build new walls to keep out prying eyes.

'Ve can't have you going through that nightmare again, can ve?' he said as he and his gang set to.

seven

Alentisk bush quivers. A stonechat, sitting on a twig, is devouring berries as Kendi and I scramble past following a dried watercourse into the mountain. It's tough going. Every kind of prickly shrub has decided to spike us. There are dozens of hedgehog plants or 'nun's pincushions', as they're called in Mallorca, and higher up tree heathers and carritx grass scratch my arms. I'm taking Kendi into the hills because she is unused to the world and frightens easily. There won't be too many dogs en route, I hope, but we seem to have got slightly lost. The path we've followed into the *torrente* is obviously a sheep track so we'll have to start to climb out soon.

Kendi doesn't stray far until we come to an almond grove or a long stretch of smooth track where she can unleash her legs and run. The pleasure she gets from expending her energy is captivating. She puts her ears back and careers off, turning as if to say 'look at me!' as she bolts, before hurtling back moments later with her reckless toothy grin.

We've come to a sheer rock face and can't find a way past so there is now no option but to lever ourselves out. Kendi's back legs are still weak from hours spent chained up, crouching in the dark, so I have to hold her round her middle and haul her over the most slippery bits. For a big dog she is surprisingly light. Soon we're on a plateau and a well-defined path but Kendi has decided to take a detour into the scrub. I can hear her barking in short sharp bursts. When I catch up she's staring at something under a bush. She swivels towards me and then, rapidly, turns back to whatever it is she's found. Come and look, she says. It's a newborn baby goat which is beginning to bleat. Another worrying call comes from somewhere higher up. On top of a rock its mother has appeared, watching us anxiously. Kendi looks from me to the mother and then back to me. What's the deal now, kiddo? Kendi's in no need of a second invitation, 'Oh, come on,' I call and she skedaddles past me up the mountain slope.

Once we're through the tree belt, the ground turns to shale and rock with little vegetation. An occasional stunted pine tree, gripping some slight and hidden nourishment from underground, is all that stands between us and Gibraltar. The panoramic view at the top is unexpected and magnificent. Over to the island of Dragonera, down to the rocks of Cala den Basset and round to the pine forests stretching the length of the sierra, there is no one in sight. Stone *casitas* dot the slopes and here and there sheep bells in the lower pastures float up on the wind. I've brought a bottle of water which I share with Kendi out of cupped hands and then, once we've marvelled at our prize, we bounce down the mountain by a different route.

There are carob trees with fresh new growth on the lower slopes. In September the carob is a two-tone tree with waxy evergreen leaves and brighter lighter foliage appearing once the deep brown pods of the carob have dropped. Once these carob beans were a valuable food source for people and animals. Now so many just lie rotting on the ground.

The aroma off the pine trees hits us first on the way down the mountain and I can hear dogs barking so I put Kendi on her lead. She's confused about her role on these walks. Should she stay and protect me or run? Being in an enclosed kennel was an easier option for her where she could be fierce knowing nothing was liable to come in after her. Out in the big wide world she's just plain scared, and sometimes so am I. Most Alsatians or Mallorquín shepherd dogs are chained or, in more remote areas, kept behind a high wire barrier to guard house and grounds but boy, when they see another dog walking by they are at their most ferocious, leaping and clawing, ready to tear us and the fence apart. Kendi does what she can, springing up and down growling and snarling at the end of the lead all along the length of the fence, which I know is mainly for my benefit because I can tell she's terrified and wants to be out of here.

I'm trying to take it in stages with her, not going too far into the hills, but even so, on a day like this, she returns to the house and flops. She has long brown toes, graceful digits, which give her an extra spring and which she plonks on my lap whenever she fancies a cuddle. Jake, meanwhile, has found a ready accommodation with Kendi. He's in charge. Just to make sure she knows who's boss, he's taken to giving her a sharp clout when she ambles past his favourite chair. Kendi, good-naturedly, skids off with a wag.

———

The men have hung their shirts on the old olive as they work on the wall. The wall is to be curved round the back of the house as Boris has ideas that I will have a swimming pool in the middle and needs it to be enclosed. He has some interesting slabs of white fossilised stone he found at the builders' merchant and wants to know if he can use it on the inside of the wall. I think it will be lovely, reminding me of a seashore, even though a swimming pool will be a long way off.

Mario is digging soil, barrowing it into a heap so that he can spread it at the base of the new wall and grow roses because, he tells me, they are a treasure trove for insects. Ants love roses, he says, because they harbour aphids and with aphids, also, come birds like nightingales. Butterflies love to drink rose nectar so all in all it's my duty to get digging. While Mario tends to the wildlife, Rafa carts cement blocks for Boris to assemble. The men have a rhythm to their work, although Rafa snatches long moments of deep sleep when he thinks no one is looking. I've often come across him, his red head resting on his shoulder, on the bench under the olive. I sometimes wonder if he is as strong as he appears.

I am preparing, bit by bit, to leave the island to cut and assemble the Juan Carlos film in the UK. I'm unable to put it off any longer although I am anxious about Kendi. She's started crying when I leave her tied up in the dark shed at night. I can hear her whining in the stillness as I walk back to the house. It is more than torture.

One evening there's a glorious sunset when Boris and his guys finish work for the day and as I walk Kendi home she resists the lead. People are out strolling in the cool air as we pass a patch of prickly pear in some rough ground. This cactus happens to be old and gangly with flat green paddles covered in malicious hairs. Nico sees us and calls out. Kendi lifts her head and takes off towards him, catching me off balance, landing me up to my neck in cactus spikes. My face, hands and legs are pierced with tiny poisonous hairs, which I can barely see yet have to somehow extract. After my earlier brush with the caterpillars, I am beyond consoling.

Nico, however, is laughing. He's amused Kendi thinks so much about him. In spite of my discomfort I can't help myself. 'Look at this lovely dog, she thinks the world of you. Why can't you let her out of the shed so that she can be with you some more?'

Nico, crestfallen, looks hurt but says quietly, 'Yes, I will do as you say,' but then, instead of letting Kendi run round, he ties her to her old kennel, she wagging her tail at him.

'But Nico, why can't you just let her be free?'

Nico says, softly, 'My father, he won't let me.'

A popular Spanish magazine, has somehow stolen pictures from my Juan Carlos film. It has managed to pirate video highlights of the movie, which it has clapped on each copy to lift sales. ITV's lawyers have been called in, there's to be a meeting with the magazine in London but the story is now out and it is stirring controversy,

For starters, the Spanish media feels it's been shafted. Here's their King, choosing to give his first interview, not to them but to me, a Brit. Arguments rage in the newspapers between the old mannered elements of Spanish society who are vehemently opposed to their King appearing like this on TV and those just itching to see what all the fuss is about. We've had to release some promotional photos to the British press that have also been plastered over every Spanish daily newspaper. There are pics of me with Juan Carlos sitting on a bench in the grounds of the Zarzuela Palace, others of us laughing on his boat and me pointing to the choke lever on his motorbike. Snooty editorials in the conservative press steam over this latest display of informal and, in their view, bad behaviour.

Meanwhile our erstwhile Spanish TV partners who had so cavalierly demanded their money back when they walked out of the deal, creep back to ask could we, please, keep quiet about their involvement. They suddenly realise that they've blown it, whether the King spoke Spanish or not, they had a scoop and it's going to make them look real dumb if news of their tantrum and their bad business decision leaks. This makes my day, and also ITV's, because it means as the controversy mounts the film grows in value and can be sold to the highest bidder.

While I'm busy working on the film trying to get it ready for airing, I'm called to London for a meeting in the gilt-edged offices of ITV's corporate lawyers to discuss tactics before the guys from the Spanish magazine arrive on the morning plane from Madrid. We're seated at an oval mahogany desk listening to the confident tones of the lawyer who has calculated the amount the magazine made out of its pirated videos and says he's going to demand in excess of £500,000 in compensation for economic loss. 'Not a cent less,' is how he puts it. Everyone nods. It all sounds right and fair.

There are three of them representing the magazine who shake hands politely and apologise for the late arrival of their plane before they're asked to join us at the oval table. Our lawyer immediately lays into them with a lecture on their appalling behaviour and a swipe at Spanish journalistic practices in general as they become more and more agitated. Finally one of the Spaniards can't hold back. 'What we've come all this way to do is to negotiate,' he shouts, 'what we're involved in here is a negotiation!'

Our lawyer tries to smooth things over, the last thing he needs is a walkout, 'Okay, okay,' he says as tempers are restored, 'all right: we're involved in a negotiation.'

For some reason the guys from the magazine remind me of the Andratx officials who wouldn't let me have electricity. I have an odd feeling these smart little suits are about to spring a surprise.

For the next six hours round that oval table the Spaniards 'negotiate' until finally one of them looks at his watch and announces. 'We have to leave, we have a plane to catch. We're going to make an offer. Ten thousand pounds. Take it or leave it,' he says.

Our guy is aghast. 'This is utterly ludicrous,' he says, but then adds, 'we'll need to talk this through with our clients, but, well, it's ridiculous.'

The Spaniard says, 'All I can tell you is if you decide you're not going to take the money you'll end up spending four or five years in a Spanish court and it's highly unlikely you'll get what you're looking for. In any case, by that time we'll have closed the magazine down and started up another, so make up your mind.'

Finally, our lawyer takes us, his exhausted clients, into another room to 'discuss' the offer but the outcome's obvious. When we return, he mutters, 'We'll take the ten thousand.'

It is difficult not to be impressed at their nerve.

With the magazine out of the way, the wrangling over whether or not the film should be shown in Spain moves up a gear as publicity continues to stoke a nationwide appetite. Eventually Spain's state broadcaster cracks, announcing it would assume 'the duty' of screening *A Year in Spain* to the Spanish public. It would broadcast on a Sunday in January, but wouldn't commit to an exact time. On the day of transmission, viewers had to hang on all day until close to midnight waiting for it. When the film finally made the airwaves, in the early hours, it recorded the biggest viewing figure for a documentary in the history of the country. And in Britain eight million people tuned in, not bad for a film ITV bosses hadn't, in the beginning, rated.

But before then I manage to take a break from cutting the film to get to Mallorca. It's November and already Mario's roses are shooting up my new wall. I'm not quite sure what colour or even what variety of rose he's planted, because he's been indulging in the usual lucky dip in the local plant nursery. The description on the ticket never matches what actually pops up. Magenta ends up as yellow, ramblers refuse to vault and although I know roses are supposed to do well in hot climates and certain climbers are better than others I'm not convinced this new planting is going to be a success. Roses seem a bit incongruous in the middle of an almond grove but it's the thought that counts.

I have been looking forward to emerging like a moth from the cocoon of my editing suite hoping to steal a bit of summer so late in the year as the months up to Christmas in the Mediterranean can be glorious. The island doesn't disappoint. On my arrival the weather is calm and serene, the kind of stillness artists crave, although any attempt to sketch the lemon tree in my garden is hijacked by Kendi's more pressing need to go exploring.

She now bounces high off the ground with all four feet, shaking her head with excitement in mid-air as we set off, her nose almost touching my heels, following my feet closely, on one of our fast romps round the mountain, past the ruined remains of the old village and the Font des Bosc, into the village by the back road. We now know, intimately, the dogs who live along the route.

Our first little friend is tied to a kennel under a palm tree on top of a terrace. He's a brown and white boxer, a lonely dog who guards a house that stands empty most of the day. He always barks a rough welcome. Kendi gives him her biggest woof in return. A little further along and it's Kendi's cue to stir up two Mallorquín shepherd dogs who rush out to warn her off, tripping over their chains each time. It is all exhilarating and, for Kendi, thirsty stuff.

Luckily the Font des Bosc is close but even though she's parched with barking, Kendi hates the cavern where spring water falls into a natural stone bowl etched out over the years. She has to crawl through creepers at the entrance and quivers and crouches, unhappy in dark places with no clear exit. I usually have to go in first and scoop out water in my hands but today for the first time, she's brave enough to attempt it on her own.

Once she's tanked up, the walk into the village is downhill and easy. A cheeky donkey in the garden of a pretty house comes trotting out as we pass by. There are banks of wild flowers and sheep grazing the fields on either side of the road. It could so easily be an English country lane although the fences here are made the old Mallorquín way from almond and wild olive branches, which weave and curl up into the hills.

All the land here and into the high Sierra was divided between the Catholic Church and the supporters of King Jaime eight hundred years ago. The same boundary lines still hold, passed on by word of mouth through the generations, marked often with just a large rock at the corner of an old stone wall.

The remains of a manorial chapel, olive mill and threshing floor stand in one of the fields. It is now deserted but was once the hub of a seigneurial way of life. In the ruins, an old, circular olive press made of granite rests on a bed of red earth. Broken from its wooden shaft, it will take a mammoth effort if ever it is to be repaired.

Once we get to the village Kendi's ears begin to swivel. A different type of dog inhabits the streets, yappy, busy little things free to do whatever takes their fancy. They spend their day checking out the opposition before returning home, worn out, for dinner.

I want to introduce Kendi to a more cosmopolitan way of life. I need her to learn about good behaviour and road etiquette. More than anything, I want her to be admired and the only way that's going to happen is if she gets out and about.

I'm starting at Sancho's because as a man of discernment he allows dogs in his café. Kendi has to learn not to go sniffing or growling after his other canine customers but there's a particular busybody, a black spaniel, who will come and pester Kendi when she's trying to be on her best behaviour.

This floppy creature barges into the bar with his big flat feet, not realising how hard it is for a dog like Kendi to be neighbourly when she's been shut off from the outside world for most of her young life. If I talk quietly and confidently to her she'll soon perk up and tell him in a low growl to mind his own business. What I must do, however, is buy Kendi a new collar so I can ditch the heavy-duty, studded affair which weighs her down and does not suit the dandy my dog has become. I want to find her one in crimson, which means a trip to the vet in the port as this is the only place around here which stocks fancy bits and bobs for dogs.

There is another vet in the district, Matias, a tall personable fellow whose surgery in Andratx opens late in the afternoon. Every bit of space in his waiting room, however, is taken with homeless kittens. There's always a cage crammed with the latest orphans on the counter. As I can't bear it, I go instead to Petra, a German vet who is also open during the day. Petra can appear a bit abrupt but her main attraction is her willingness to lend out her cat trap, an oblong contraption with a metal plate at its entrance. When a feral cat spies a lump of fresh meat and ventures in, it puts its foot on the plate, snapping shut a door behind it. Although fearsome, the trap is a godsend when there are so many uncatchable cats in need of help.

Petra was bequeathed hers by an animal charity, and she is extremely possessive of it. I've always got to jump a queue of patients meowing in crates and a posse of stray cats queueing for breakfast outside her backstreet surgery if I want to get my hands on the trap.

The first time I desperately needed it was the morning I'd fed four cute Siamese kittens who'd made their home in a back garden in the village. They were playing when out from under a rampant passionflower crawled a young ginger cat. As he clambered slowly towards me, I couldn't, honestly, believe my eyes. He had been so badly torn in a fight his entrails were hanging out. Even now, I can't quite describe the condition he was in; it was heartbreaking. And yet, in spite of his mortal injuries, he was yowling for something to eat. I gave him what I had and immediately set off to the port to find Petra.

At first she was reluctant to lend someone she didn't know her cat trap, uncertain if she would see it again, but after I begged, she relented. Unfortunately, when I got back, the cat had gone so I had to wait for what seemed an eternity, with the cage and a piece of fresh chicken, hoping he'd reappear. Half an hour later, he was back, his little face screwed up. He smelled the food and didn't hesitate. He limped into the cage. Now I had the gruesome job of getting him into the car and back to Petra as he fought manically to break free.

A young Mallorquín, I remember, came over to help, shaking his head when he saw what I'd got. He went to find an old towel to drape over the cage to give a bit of comfort to the creature now wailing inside.

Outside Sancho's a couple of English women gossiping over coffee also came to see what was happening. They turned away when they saw what I'd got inside. It was left to me to take the cat back to Petra who made me watch as she administered the final injection. It was her way, she said, of making people take responsibility. As if I needed any lesson in that.

———

The year Kendi with her new red necklace became a fixture in my life I got a black, shiny motorbike, which took me down quiet roads with the wind and sun in my face and all the way to Palma to the salvage yard, before it came to a sticky end when it ran into a boulder on my rocky road. I'd heard about the Chimney Place from Boris who bought most of his second-hand building materials there. It is located in the gypsy quarter of Palma, on the way to Manacor. Small, square houses with washing on roofs line the streets and, heedless of traffic, dirty children dart in and out.

Finding the Chimney Place is relatively easy if I can keep my eye on the tall brick chimney towering above the dereliction. It marks a gold mine of old stone sinks, marble pillars, floor tiles stacked hundreds high, mahogany doors and windows, chairs and tables, all taken from the old homes, palaces and churches of Palma. There must be four large warehouses stuffed with artefacts scavenged during the rampant demolition of old Palma, row upon row of solid pitch pine doors and windows and scruffy sofas from once wealthy households, now well-sprung beds for stray cats and their litters of kittens.

From the Chimney Place I bought old mosaic blue and white tiles, a stone sink, windows, doors and all manner of implements, which I hung on walls or incorporated one way or another in my house. For me it was a magnet, a marvelling at lost architectural gems stacked so wantonly in this grubby backyard. My bike was able to get me there fast for a recce and once I'd found something I couldn't resist I'd put down a deposit and return with a car to pick it up later. I'd got the bug.

From the flea market in Palma held every Saturday at five in the morning I bought large glazed olive oil jars. Swarthy, bulky men with leathered skin commandeered every street corner leading to the cathedral, selling gear they'd obviously nicked. Doing business with these vagabonds, haggling over church antiques, gilt angels and crosses or oil paintings of biblical scenes, was like dealing with so many menacing desecrating devils. I got so I couldn't.

I could, however, shop at the flea market in the wine village of Consell on the way to Inca, the principal town of Mallorca's central plain. Here was a totally different and fun deal. Firstly, it was on a Sunday and you didn't have to be there so early. And secondly, a trip to Consell meant a pit stop first at the market of Santa Maria. This was another experience I wanted Kendi to savour. Santa Maria del Cami, to give it its full name, is an ancient Roman town on the main thoroughfare to the north, which in late medieval times developed its own a slave trade. The Moors who followed the Romans made the town one of their principal settlements. It has always been a gathering place for the island. There are piles of welcoming cafés on the main road which look out on an impressive seventeeth-century monastery: the Monestir de Nostra Senyora de la Soledad, its cloister just glimpsed through wrought-iron gates in honey-coloured high stone walls.

Kendi is getting very partial to ensaimadas and café living where she can sit and be served in the sunshine. She takes a piece of ensaimada gently now and chews it in appreciation. I think she prefers, out of all the ensaimadas in Mallorca, the ones made here in this town.

The market spills out round the church a few streets away. On a Sunday a colourful, glorious Mallorca of tomatoes, aubergines, grapes, honey, nuts and flowers blazes in the sun. Melons are sliced with lethal knives as the price of gingols (a rosy and prolific fruit) swiftly reaches the crowd.

I'm here for the honey stall. Bees are big business in markets across the island. Thousands of beehives produce a ton of honey from two main crops a year. First comes the spring flower honey, *mille fleurs*. Then comes the heavier duty carob honey from the carob trees in November, on All Saints' Day. It is stickier and more substantial and not as sweet. What I want to find is rosemary, '*romero*' honey or perhaps honey from the almond blossoms, gathered just after the flowers have faded. *Miel d'Romero* is my favourite, spooned over goat's yoghurt or poured on warm figs when they are in season. It is hard to concentrate on which out of the many varieties of honey I should buy from Santa Maria today, there's a lot of laughter ricocheting and amplifying through the town's narrow streets.

Many homes in Santa Maria have pine branches hanging over front doors in various stages of dehydration, as though someone has forgotten to take down Christmas decorations. These branches signal wine fermentation going on in darkened cellars along almost every street. The browner and drier the branch, the readier the wine fermenting underground. Santa Maria is right in the middle of the wine-growing area of the island but prefers to leave the industrial stuff to other towns. Wine here is personal. Families use their cellars to brew their own and a drying pine branch above the door lets everyone know when it's time to party.

Kendi's first experience of an island market wasn't a happy one. I walked her once to Andratx market where she took on the look of a wolf hunting her prey, pushing up against the heavy bottoms of local ladies as they queued three deep at the stalls. No one dared pat her, but once she'd got weary with the effort and commotion, she relaxed and, although not wildly joyous, she at least managed to buck up a bit and half-heartedly trot, less menacingly, along.

Today in Santa Maria, she's cool, so once I've loaded my basket with fresh fruit we're ready to set about the flea market in Consell, a mile or so up the road. Consell also makes wine and has a well-known local bread they call pa moreno, a dark rye baked in a wood oven which forms the basis of the simple pa amb oli and so many other Mallorquín peasant dishes. Consell – like other towns in the central plain, Santa Maria and Binissalem – surprises with its beautiful homes in its central square, built by wealthy wine merchants at a time when Mallorca exported fine wines to Europe. These houses are discreet, crafted from golden stone with impressive olive wood front doors and cellars and courtyards furnished with family antiques.

The flea market is on the outskirts of Consell, in the grounds of a nut factory where stalls stack up next to a growing pile of almond husks used for fuel in the winter months. In summer crowds engulf stalls selling iron keys and bolts, or rummage in once neat bundles of embroidered linen. There is no shade here. It's scorching. In the winter months I've bought rolls of striped grey cotton army twill which I've had made into cushions and covers for my chairs outside. One day I also staggered back with a pine harrow, an agricultural implement made from a large flat board, which had embedded in it sharpened flints set in perfect rows. I hung it on my sitting room wall. This morning, as Kendi is with me, we're in a socialising mood, which means we stop and wag tails or give a quick sideways growl to a dodgy pooch or two.

Sometimes, after a Sunday market at Consell I'll make for the country restaurant Cellar Sa Sini, on the corner of the main road back in Santa Maria. It doesn't open until one but by half past the beamed Mallorquín dining room is packed with local families chirping, building for their happy Sunday lunch. The food is home cooked, and the puddings tempting. It is also cheap, as is the wine served from the imposing oak barrels lining the walls. If I'm with friends, rosado is a favourite. It's a potent cross between blanco and tinto that arrives in a bottle uncorked that, once emptied, is recycled, topped up for the next customer.

Summer or winter the restaurant is always inviting. In winter a log fire burns in the vaulted fireplace as warming dishes of arroz brut, sopas Mallorquín or frito Mallorquín trundle from the kitchen along with something called a 'stew of meets'. In summer a cooling fountain flowing down the outer walls of the restaurant makes eating in the courtyard a pleasure for bikers and locals alike.

A Mallorquín family is waiting in the courtyard in the sunshine, the window of the restaurant flung open behind them. Grandpa is wearing his best cloth cap; Grandma, their daughter and son-in-law are busy with a boisterous four-year-old. They're at a table and the child is running round screaming. I can see the grandfather is irritated, trying to galvanise his daughter, who's gossiping with her mother, into applying a bit of discipline. She can't. The child has now barged into the restaurant, climbed on the window ledge and taken to throwing almonds at Grandpa, who, angry, only makes his grandson bolder, inadvertently thumping Grandpa in the ear when he tries to swipe his cap off his head. Grandpa jumps up, dives through the window, grabs his grandson and wallops him across the bottom. The child's mother carries on as though none of this is happening but the boy quietens, I notice, and all through lunch sits silently by his grandfather's side, both of them suddenly extremely well behaved.

It's very much a grown-up pastime this sitting around on pavements. Local people, especially on a summer evening, prop chairs outside their front doors one next to the other in a long line to get air and to gossip, saying how '*mucho calor*', how hot is the night, something now remarked upon when once it wasn't. I think everyone agrees the summers are getting hotter but how any of them can happily sit on a pavement, anyway, their chairs wobbling as traffic thunders past, is always puzzling.

I've been on the island months now and still have not yet made the sea crossing to mysterious Dragonera about five miles off the coast of San Telm, where King Jaime and his great fleet first ran for cover in the thirteenth century. At sunset Dragonera casts a spell over Mallorca, rippling the ocean, stirring shadows, as the last rays of the day dip down. There is always an audience on the jetty in San Telm as the final curtain comes down in the west.

Apparently Jaime didn't plan to conquer Mallorca from the waters off San Telm. He had been on his way to Pollensa in the north but a wind blowing from Provence stirred up such an enormous storm he had to change course. Jaime had also heard about a spring of fresh water on the island of Dragonera so made for it instead.

He wasn't the only one who's dropped anchor there. A thousand years before, so legend has it, Noah sailed in to repopulate the land. Now no one inhabits the island, although there was once a large estate with a lovely garden at its southern end where peacocks and exotic varieties of pheasant were reared. Soon after I bought my house this completely natural island, as Jaime – and Noah for that matter – would have remembered it, was purchased by the government to save it from developers. It is called Dragonera because in profile it looks like a recumbent dragon and it's been luring me to visit for ages.

Cedric knows a guy who's just had a refit on his boat and is putting it through its paces by taking it to Dragonera. He's told him I'd like to come along for the ride. It's early and I'm in the port being welcomed aboard a white plastic cruiser by Luigi, an elderly guy who apparently is big in textiles in Italy. His mechanic is an English boy, Rick, and also on board is Rick's mongrel, a dog called Pip. Soon we're powering out to sea, the men listening to the sound of the motor while I lounge on the brow, warm air blasting as the boat skids across the waves.

Dragonera has three lighthouses, one abandoned and two at either end of the island which still flash their vital intermittent light over the black waters. I plan to walk to the derelict lighthouse at its highest point on Na Popia so we steer towards a landing spot at Cala Llado on Dragonera where I'll be dropped off and collected later for a picnic lunch while the guys go off on more sea trials.

It is an easy walk, following a broad footpath built by prisoners who had been brought over to construct the lighthouse in the nineteenth century. There is no one around this early, so I have Dragonera to myself, well almost. Out of every shrub and rock there are little lizards. I have never seen so many, there must be millions of them shooting in and out. These lizards are called sargantana and are indigenous to Mallorca. They have no fear but pop up, then freeze, playing games of hide and seek in the heat. There is lots of rosemary and wild olive and cistus, a typically Mediterranean landscape wonderfully unwrecked, and by the time I reach the heights of the island I feel disorientated, unable to comprehend how neatly Dragonera has managed to duck development.

From Na Popia the view of the ocean and the island's vertical cliffs is staggering. There are hawks everywhere, rare Elenora's falcons catching the currents, soaring high, gracefully sweeping the cliff edge. They nest here before migrating to Madagascar for the winter. Lucky birds.

When I get back the boat is anchored a little way off the shore. Rick is in the water with his mongrel, doggy-paddling beside him. The sun is high and the water inviting. Like an eager mermaid, slipping from the rocks into the depths, I'm soon at the boat and aboard. Luigi is pleased with the speed and sound of the engine so he's gone off on a more gentle amble to the southern lighthouse and will be back soon.

Rick and his dog only have eyes for one another. Rick tells me the usual tale of how he found Pip tied without shade in the hot sun and starving when he was working on a building site. He sneaked back one night, cut Pip's chain and took him. Pip now follows him everywhere. 'But what if you have to go back to England? ' I want to know. 'You'll have to put him in quarantine or leave him behind.'

Rick shrugs. 'I'm going back soon,' he says, 'and Pip's coming with me. I can't afford quarantine. I'll smuggle her in on a boat. Everyone does it.' Pip gazes up adoringly.

Luigi, back from his walk, shouts from the shore for Rick to coax the boat to the jetty. There's just time for our picnic and afterwards, with the hot sun directly overhead, we start the engine and bounce wildly back over the waves to the Port.

It is because of the sensation of a cool sea in a hot summer that I've started day-dreaming about a swimming pool at the house. Boris has been clever, of course, leaving me enough space in the centre of his high stone wall. The thought of slinking into my own pool on a July night is ridiculous of course.

How can I ever contemplate such a thing when I don't have electricity?

Only a couple of weeks after my trip to Dragonera the mountain behind my house begins to glow. It has a strange orange halo over it and I can't quite work out why. These July days have been impossibly hot, made worse by a dry wind blowing from the Sahara, parching the grasses and unsettling the animals in the fields. Now it is night, the wind hasn't fallen and the sky flares and falters in the west. It must be a forest fire; it can't be anything else. There is nothing between me and the coast except thousands of hectares of pine trees and scrub. Somewhere in there a fire has begun.

Friends who have come to stay are getting edgy. They are in their bedroom, nervously watching the mountain as smoke begins to fill the valley sucking the smell of burning towards us. They have to leave, they say, fearing if they don't go soon, they'll be trapped.

The strength of the blaze, I've decided, must be colossal. The orange glow has now turned glossy crimson as the mountain on fire appears to pulsate. 'Perhaps if I get you to the airport I'll be able to get back here to see what can be done,' I suggest. They don't hesitate, now desperate to get away from the flames wrapping the hill.

Thankfully Kendi is in her kennel, out of the valley, but I'm worried about Jake. I need to catch him and get him to safety, but as I load up the car Jake doesn't respond. I pray he's in the house, hiding from me, as usual.

I'm at the airport and back in under an hour as villagers arrive to help. It's a fire at the monastery of Sa Trapa, they say, and it's spreading fast, heading to the valley. It won't be long before it reaches the village. In the glow from the distant blaze, I can make out Mario and some other fit young men who have turned up, nerved to act. They have scythes and other sharp implements and are making for the far side of the nearest hill to try and cut a fire path through the scrub, to attempt to block the route of the flames. They have to do something, they say, and can they take my chainsaw, which is hanging in my garden shed?

The police, the Guardia Civil, has barricaded the track to prevent people getting too close, but this hasn't stopped those on foot circumnavigating to offer support. We're hearing there are fires all over Spain. A blaze on Ibiza has meant one of the two planes scrambled to fight our fire has had to be diverted. The Canary Islands also have massive forest fires. Mainland seaplanes have been sent there. All we've been left are volunteers from the village and the local fire brigade, whose vintage engine has taken up position outside Lauren's home. It has no access to any water.

The young couple with a baby who have rented Lauren's house for the summer have taken fright and driven off. Gunther and Francine are out in the valley, so too are Emmy Lou and her friend Joleen who, having taken a rake from my shed, are marching up the road following Mario. I can hear horses in the fields higher up, whinnying. I still can't find Jake in the commotion but if I leave the doors of the house open, hopefully he'll come in, soon, for cover. Panic is building as the fire, now uncontrollable, begins showering ash.

I'm finding it hard to remain inactive, behind the police barrier, waiting for the worst. The knowledge that Mallorca is so ill-equipped to deal with a catastrophe like this is incomprehensible. Soon the fire will be on us. I cannot hang around any longer so I catch up with Mario and the guys on the north slope of the next hill, who are hacking back dried branches and rangy shrubs. The men are speedily working in an organised line clearing a way through the pines. Emmy Lou is standing with the rake, like Boadicea, watching as Mario frantically breaks branches with his hands trying to halt the impending devastation. Another young man is using my chainsaw to slice through a tree which together we manage to roll further down the hill.

Suddenly there are shouts that a helicopter has arrived with a bucket to douse flames. The wind has also started to back down. No one is sure what to do next, it could be dangerous for those of us exposed on the hill so quickly we all move to leave, reaching the valley bottom just as hell descends.

I have never been so close or seen or heard anything in my life quite like it. The wind having backed, suddenly decided to veer again, sending the fire raging over the high mountain top down into the *torrente* towards us. The flames, which were now funnelled, charged past the sheer slopes of the valley, tumbling and growing, exploding over every tree. The fireball then leapt up, took out the hillside we had just been working on, and then suddenly retreated. What happened in those few minutes was remarkable, the wind had changed direction several times in a couple of minutes, finally whipping round to drive the fire away, away from the valley but searing those standing close by as it passed.

Now, however, we had help: a sole helicopter was on the case. He clattered over the valley with a bucket slung under the fuselage which he targeted on the blaze. Back and forth he flew to *cisternas* in the village, taking up water to finish off patches of fire which kept surfacing on the hill. All night long the pilot worked, beyond all safety limits, ferrying water until only plumes of curly black smoke remained.

As dawn broke that morning, the air remained grey in the burned-out almond groves. Skeletons of ancient olives, hundreds of years old, smouldered on for weeks, the fire at their heart fed by the oil in their sap. On the hill we had tried to protect, stone walls once lost in vegetation, now stood clear, along with traces of time-worn footpaths. Everything else had gone, leaving a stark hillside delineated with the bare terraces of centuries long gone. I didn't think then, but certainly realised now as I looked at the force the blaze had wrought in minutes how stupid I had been to fight this fire and how close I had come to losing my life.

'Monster Forest Fire Horror, Homes Evacuated in Selina

Scott's village' said the local paper that day, but for me the horror was in the loss of my lovely cat, Jake. Jake never returned that night or the following morning, although I looked everywhere in the house for him, under the beds, in the bread oven, climbing the hill to see if he was hiding somewhere. There was no sight and no sound. In the days following I searched and searched, eventually advertising for his return. In an island inundated with stray cats, it was a forlorn hope. I never saw Jake again but in my better moments tried to believe he had charmed his way into someone's house and they were now caring for him as much as I did. Even so, I never lost hope that I might find him again.

As for the saviour of the valley, the helicopter pilot, who gave so much in such frightening circumstances, a thanksgiving celebration was laid on in his honour. The women, Emmy Lou among them, cooked and baked and organised. On the day, however, a Saturday, our hero was held up and, arriving late, discovered that the banquet had gone, it had been eaten up. Fine words were all that were left, along with a couple of sausage rolls.

The forest fire was a disaster for Mallorca. Although everyone was convinced the fire had been started deliberately in the old monastery of Sa Trapa, the fact that the island, in spite of its wealth, couldn't deliver equipment to cope with an emergency on this scale became a trigger for action. A new fleet of spotter planes began patrolling the summer skies looking for fire, signs went up over the island warning against the use of matches, and a local law forbidding bonfires in the summer months came into force. Vigilance had finally taken hold, although it was too late for the mature pine forests and old olive groves that had informed the beauty of this part of the island. Now, for miles along the western coast, the stumps of pines jagged on the slopes punctuated this area of outstanding natural beauty.

In all the anger following the fire, perhaps the only person to feel a certain satisfaction was Gunther. For years he had been castigated for letting his goats wander the valley stripping the ground of plants until it turned brown and bare. Now was his moment. If it hadn't been for the goats clearing the hills of a fire hazard, Gunther regaled, none of us or our homes would be here today.

eight

eight

Unfortunately Carter seems to have killed my plum tree with his heavy-handed pruning. The haircut obviously hurt. The tree started weeping heavy drops of sap out of every cut in January and by June it was dead. I never saw Carter again. If I had I'd have scalped him. Soon after the massacre of my hundred-year-old plum, Carter left Mallorca to take up horticulture in Mexico. His mother, Emmy Lou, cooed how Carter, her talented boy, was particularly gifted with plants.

After the forest fire I returned to work, travelling to the US to set up my next project, a documentary on a secret journey King Constantine was planning to Greece to give his young family the chance to experience a summer in a homeland none of them had ever known and which he hadn't visited for longer than twenty-four hours in twenty-five years. We would fly to mainland Greece and then board a boat to sail through the Aegean, a trip which promised fireworks because the King, exiled after a military coup a quarter of a century back, had decided not to tell the Greek Government of Mitsotakis he was returning. It was, to say the least, an audacious move by this ex-head of state, who knew he was not at all welcome. To conduct, all these years later, an undercover mission to the country of which he was once King was pretty obviously the stuff of headlines. Not that ITV, who commissioned my documentaries, saw it that way. They simply could not envisage why anyone outside Greece would be interested.

Which was just as well. I had a feeling there'd be firecrackers and wasn't particularly keen on stirring up another media storm in the UK so soon after the film on Spain. When America with an eye to its massive Greek population snapped up the idea instead and assigned me two crews, I felt oddly relieved. If there was to be a fuss better it be Stateside.

With my itinerary now sorted, and just before filming began, I managed to get back to Mallorca.

It is getting so I don't know what to expect when I turn up after a few weeks away, but on the balmy morning of my arrival I am thrilled to see Kendi running round her enclosure. Nico is with her, feeding the goats, ducks and chickens, happy to tell me he always lets her off her chain so she is able to stretch her legs. What a turnaround. When Kendi spots me she does cartwheels, vociferously letting me know, as if I don't already, that it's great to have me back and for God's sake, get me out of here. Nico doesn't seem to mind this exuberance, he's laughing as he goes to get her lead so that soon Kendi and I, together, career up the track, she with unfettered pleasure, towards my shuttered house.

While Kendi canters round the field, I wade through the debris of dropped petals and leaves to unlock the door and let the sun shine in. More than anything, the smell of this house, when the doors creak open after a time away, is immediately soothing. I think it has to do with old stones and oiled wood absorbing heat that penetrates through the floors and roof, mixing with the lavender hanging in bunches from the beams. It is just like being in an old oak cradle.

Except this time, Jake isn't here. I miss the adorable Jake most of all in the mornings, but through the tears I have decided there'll be no more cats coming to live here, adept at worming their way into my life, desperate to be my one true friend. I can hardly blame the breed of cat that inhabits this island. Apparently Mallorquín cats came over on boats from Egypt centuries back, the kind of cat Cleopatra might have had with their regal profile and intelligence. When I hear of kindly folk in other parts of the island who start off feeding a few and end up coping with dozens, like Emmy Lou once did, it keeps me awake at night.

Luckily and blessedly, Pepita in the village has stepped in to help feed the Siamese kittens living in the garden next door.

She knows them well, as there were once thirteen. She got landed when her neighbour died and his two pet Siamese were turfed out. Over the years these two cats brought back litter after litter for Pepita to feed. Only five from this original family have survived, all with creamy coats, smudgy black and brown paws and eyes of ice. The father of this brood prowls his territory beating off interlopers while the mother cat feeds and sleeps with her kittens, all curled round one another, in a discarded metal trunk. This is her second batch of kittens in a year. The first all perished so I know if I don't feed them and stop the females getting pregnant this latest litter won't last a winter. It's not what I would have wished my first task back on the island to be, particularly as I don't have much time, but some things can't wait. I have to tackle their father, the big tom, first.

Sancho is in his backyard sorting crates when I show up with the cat trap again, baited with a morsel of chicken. Tom cat, who has sharp eyes in a broad head, is all of a swagger but when he saunters up to sniff the chicken he somehow senses trouble. He pads round, paws the cage, jumps on it, shaking it with his sudden weight, and then shoots off as the trap suddenly clanks shut. Sancho starts to chuckle from behind his crates of empty bottles.

Plan B. I reckon the piece of chicken isn't tempting enough. If I was a greedy male I'd need more than a morsel to get my juices going, so I'm back to the butcher for a whole half. If this doesn't get him in, nothing will. When Mr Tom eventually reappears his nose is twitching. He marches straight up, can't believe the chunk sitting there and rushes in. He's caught. The door has banged tight behind him. As the cage spins up into the air, tom cat turns into a tiger, snarling and spitting to be out. Sancho reappears and calls out '¡El gato, magnifico!' But it is too late. 'Oh, tragico, muy, muy tragico,' he moans as tom cat and I head to Petra.

It didn't take long and I'm sure it didn't hurt because Tom is raring to go after his quick nip, catapulting into the plumbago on his release. When he shows up again it isn't with malice. He gobbles and growls as I dole out his food and carries on beating off all cats who dare put a paw on his patch. He certainly hasn't lost all his *cojones*.

The rest of his gang I manage to collar in the days ahead and when Pepita offers to feed them when I'm away, I feel this little family has finally been given a fighting chance.

My coming and going from Mallorca makes me do things I would never contemplate if I lived full-time on the island. Like finally building a swimming pool, for which I blame Boris totally. His arty walls, made with a pool in mind, enclosed a space which when he'd finished looked bereft. The roses faltered. Planted against a south-facing wall in heavy clay, they couldn't cope with the scorching sun, but it was the cracks in the new walls that finally did for me. What began as hairline fissures soon sprouted ants' nests, which sent their inhabitants swarming up and over everything. The ants branched out into the rangy roses, they tunnelled under the clay, emerging every now and again carrying an egg in their front claws to kick off yet another nursery in a more spacious residence further up the line. It was as though Boris had built the wall especially for these resourceful creatures. There was nothing for it but to build a new cool blue pool and move the wagon train on.

Except Boris has gone to ground. He has another project, he conveniently announces, the reconstruction of an old corn mill which will take many years to complete. I think he guesses what lies ahead. So Mario, Rafa and Carlos disappear up another dirt track to the top of a nearby mountain where a similar derelict bolthole beckons. Only Cedric is offering to stay, as long as someone else digs the hole, because Cedric's out of the game for a while. He's broken his leg tripping over the dog.

Can you build me a pool this year? I ask Ignacio Ramirez, another local builder. Yes. Are you certain it will be ready for next summer? Of course. And what about electricity? Do you think I will ever manage to get a supply to my house? Yes, definitely. I will do this for you. You will? Will it be soon? Yes. Are you sure? Absolutely.

One of the most disconcerting traits of a Mallorquín is his ability to never tell you the truth straight up. I now know this; I didn't then. I think it has something to do with politeness and not wishing to offend. So he doesn't say 'no' but instead procrastinates by telling you 'yes'.

And so it was I decided to go ahead with the mad folly of making a pool without a proper source of power. Do you think the generator will work the jets to circulate the water? Of course. How long will I have to run it to keep the pool clean? *Oh, mas o menos, quatra horas* (more or less four hours). Are you absolutely sure? Yes. There will be no problem.

I have been hearing about this young builder, who has started his own construction firm, employing local craftsmen to service a flood of Germans desperate to spend cash fast on high-quality homes in the sun. Ignacio is getting quite a repu- tation for work built to last, as demands for only the best push up local standards. The attraction Germany feels for Spain is not only mutual but mirrored. A rigorous, driven energy emanating from the north reflects in a warm, laissez-faire approach to life here in Mallorca, which lends each an appre- ciation of the opposite qualities of the other. Spain, with its hands on the money, has gone mad for Mercs and Volks- wagens and all things Deutsch. Germany, dishing out the readies, has bought into the dreamy glow of a long Mediter- ranean embrace demanding, on the way, perfection. Ignacio, who has just returned from Granada in mainland Spain with a psychology degree, obviously feels equipped for the chal- lenge so after a while I decide he might be just the man to build a pool, against all the odds, for me.

Ignacio is like a little black charger. I phone to make an appointment or as he calls it 'a meet' and on the dot of the hour, I can hear his jeep careering up the track. This is very unusual in Mallorca but Ignacio is determined to be different and show his new clients he doesn't buy bad Spanish time-keeping. His King, Juan Carlos, would be proud of him

Ignacio strides over the parched earth in his Timberland boots taking the steps to the patio in one bound, locking his big brown eyes on the business deal ahead. He's wearing chinos and a polo shirt, dressed ruggedly, pumping my hand as he asks, seriously, after my health. He speaks English fluently, so my Spanish pronunciation and exaggerated hand gestures – as though I'm talking to a Chinese waiter who doesn't understand – are for once superfluous. He is quick to agree that the area defined by the walls has to be made lovely and affirms that a pool couldn't be put in a better place. He will need to get a licence and work out dimensions but he is enthusiastic. As we investigate the cracks in the wall, however, he starts tutting, shaking his head, saying he would-n't have been allowed to build walls in the 'backside' like this, with no foundations. 'No foundations? Surely not.'

Ignacio, sensing my mood, quickly backtracks. Not to worry, he blithely reassures, it can be fixed. *No problemas*.

No foundations. *No problemas*. I feel sick. To think all this work over all these months and I've been so stupid I didn't notice or question. I might have guessed the walls were going up too damned fast. And here I am with another build-ing project. A swimming pool, which will end up who knows where, built by another cast of characters of who knows what ability.

Cedric is not in a helpful frame of mind. He's loyal to Boris, of course, but his plaster cast is slowing him down and he is bad-tempered. It was one of the dogs he rescued off the roadside that led to his downfall. It, Bozo, was lying on top of the stairs when Cedric got up in the night to go to the downstairs loo. Dottie had been on at Cedric for ages to fix a handrail to the stairs but Cedric, being Cedric, didn't. Next thing, he'd stumbled out of bed and, not seeing a recumbent hound lying on the top stair, tripped and fallen badly down to the stone floor below. He moaned and groaned for hours but Dottie, thinking she was hearing the dogs mumbling in their sleep, didn't get up. Cedric was lucky he lived. Dottie reckons it was the vino in the bar earlier that night that saved him, made him so relaxed he bounced rather than crashed.

Cedric's house is a bit like Steptoe's but with a wonderful view. It looks out over the valley as an eagle might, except Cedric's nest is in a rare state of decrepitude. His kitchen has been rigged up outside under a tarpaulin because he has no electricity. A rusty cooker, fridge and barbecue entertain in all weathers Cedric's happy band of guitar-playing brothers – his mates down the pub – who gather under the stars for al fresco nights. All around a fine collection of old sinks, doors, windows, tin sheets, taps and scrap motorbikes spill out up and over the hill because Cedric is also an inveterate rounder-upper of stuff other people have thrown out.

Tuesday, being bin day in the village, is rich in old bits and bobs locals don't rate. They pile it all up by the big green plastic bins on the verge, which is then carted off on the back of a lorry to the tip down the road. In fact, nothing ever gets moved that far because most is recycled by sharp-eyed locals. I've picked up a large Indian rug and a mahogany wardrobe, which took some shifting, but with a bit of cleaning and polishing now adorns my house. Cedric goes round the bins with his seven-year-old son Jim in an old pick-up truck. It must be a great education for a youngster.

Cedric doesn't have social security so the encounter with his dog is costing him. It is a real worry for once carefree fellows like him who now have families to look after. Cedric, however, has another emporium in a backstreet in Andratx, where he trades second-hand gear, electrical and plumbing equipment for DIYers or boat owners. Dottie, of course, has to pitch in and help sometimes as a grumpy plumber's mate. I daren't contemplate how long the pool is going to take to build if my chief electrician remains off his legs for long.

———

Kendi, at least, is a joyful distraction to the ongoing dramas of village life. There can't be a day when I'm in residence that she doesn't come with me. In any case, she now knows my footfall and gets into a frenzy if she hears I'm heading her way. The thought of her anchored to a chain galvanises me to walk long distances. She's getting better at meeting people and is now on her doggy best behaviour when we slope off to look in folks' back gardens. She knows if she spots another dog behind a fence she has to appear superior and not engage in rough brawls. Her ears go awry as she quickly determines if the mutt making the noise in a yard is worth a put-down woof or not. She has now learned that a dog wagging a tail heading in our direction is usually of the friendly persuasion.

On one of my first trips in the village with Kendi, a cuddly golden retriever ambled up and she nearly took his head off, thinking, I guess, he was about to attack me. Now she knows the drill I take her regularly into the tapestry of orchards and vegetable plots, snooping round the little village houses in the back lanes. Linking these houses are tiny footpaths that meander through almond groves tripping over old stone walls before emerging in someone's front garden. This is where the older people of the village live, where vines smother pergolas and cobbled paths are weeded. Hanging bunches of luscious grapes are wrapped and tied in newspaper, and cotton curtaining that protects olive wood front doors bleaches in the sun. Most of the village houses are lived in by local people who regularly lime-wash their arched front doors and windows to keep out insects. And always they sport the same bright green shutters. There are lots of small, bug-eyed dogs living in pet heaven here, lurking behind well-stacked piles of logs along with the occasional parrot screeching from its cage hung in the open air.

There's an old stone water trough down one of the side streets which will once have been the hub of village life, now most gardens have their own *cisternas*, filled with spring water that gets poured on lemons and oranges and beans and tomatoes in the hot months. Late in the year, before the rains come, mounds of rich red earth are scraped back from the base of every plant and tree so that nothing misses out on a good soak. Orange trees are worth every ounce of effort. Their scent envelops the valley and hangs in the air for weeks at blossom time.

To the north of the village the land gets mountainous, inhabited mainly by hippies and artists and a few local people who spend weekends repairing family smallholdings. To the south and west is a richer, flatter landscape where a different kind of folk altogether, the Village Raj, have taken up residence in kitted-out homes with plentiful underground water. Most of these ex-pats arrived in the 1950s at the end of the Second World War, fleeing the austerity of a post-war Europe but unable to entirely forgo an English way of life where Radio 4, Earl Grey tea, dinner parties and periodicals sent from Britain still bolster a sunnier existence. Bristling in the middle of these ex-naval commanders, minor aristocrats and code breakers from Bletchley, are some old Nazis and a scattering of Cold War spies.

A single-track road ventures through this wonderland teeming with wild flowers, orchids, poppies, buttercups, shepherd's purse and tightly guarded houses, patrolled by dogs and lived in by people who keep to themselves. Kendi is always a bit skittish accompanying me on this walk. She has never encountered such menacing hounds before, like the

Dobermans who bare their teeth, spraying spittles of slaver through the mesh of the high wire fence shielding who knows what clandestine affair.

There must be at least six radio masts in the garden of this house, poking out from behind cypress trees, reaching to the heavens. I imagine an SS commandant once stationed on the icy Russian Front, in there, somewhere, communicating from his sunny garden across the globe to his pals in the southern hemisphere. I bet he hasn't the foggiest that one of his near neighbours, an ex-Wren once based at Bletchley, is a whizz at cracking radio signals. She and her ex-navy husband live a richly retired life only a few doors away. She was so expert at deciphering German battle codes she relayed them directly to Winston Churchill. I'd be very tempted to keep my hand in if I were her, doing a bit of eavesdropping on the side.

Further down the road and adding *joie de vivre* to all the intrigue is a beautiful painterly garden, which might have graced an aristocratic summer house in the south of France in the 1930s. A finca washed in ochre looks out on to planting which reflects the colours of the sun and sky. Kendi once went wandering down its open driveway to see what she could see and came across a sliver of paradise teeming with roses and geranium and jasmine. Eight magnificent cypress trees led the eye to an horizon greened with a perfectly trimmed lawn, but a little black cat suddenly spat from its sunny perch on a low wall and Kendi didn't hang around.

It's fascinating how attractive island life is to operatives of one sort or another. Anthony, a tall middle-aged American, Harvard educated and a former CIA agent, lives here with his wife Jen in a quietly distinguished house. He naturally has a fondness for a fine Scotch malt, preferably Laphroig, and when I asked him once in the bar what brought him to live permanently in this tiny village he said he didn't know what on earth possessed him to come to this 'one-horse town', but 'all I know is I don't want to be anywhere else'.

Greville Wynne, the British spy who was imprisoned in the infamous Lubyanka prison in the Soviet Union, and was finally released at the Berlin Wall in exchange for the Soviet spy, Gordon Lonsdale, had a yearning for the Mediterranean and ended up in Palma growing roses.

These twists to the end of a life that has witnessed turbulence and brutality appeal to both the journalist and romantic in me. To think of Greville Wynne desiring to purge the sickness of a Soviet gaol with the scent of flowers in Mallorca makes my own small quest for a bit of peace here unquestionably tame.

As Kendi and I are intent on having breakfast in the port we have to leave this valley in all its subterfuge and climb a track worn to the rock with the cartwheels of old. It is a bit of an effort but the view from the first set of hills encircling the village is magical. A haze has settled over the valley but through it you can make out the houses and gardens we've just walked past as if they've been swathed in silk. I could spend hours with a pair of binoculars here, but a dog – and particularly Kendi – isn't up for something as boring as this. We have to keep moving.

The track goes on to the coast but Kendi and I set off on a diversion, its location takes some remembering. To miss it means we'll spend hours lost in scratchy scrub but today we get it right, boulders mark our way, so that soon we're climbing almost vertically to a grass ledge to finally rest a little under a mighty, overhanging cliff face, the mountains and coast spread before us. Like so many paths in Mallorca this one turns out not to be as daunting as it looks. There's a chasm in the rock face and through it, innocently, the path takes us on to another level, a high plateau where we join a well-defined track all the way to the port. Kendi leaps along easily with the new-found strength in her legs, the village shimmering on our left, the sea shining on our right.

Soon we're near our destination, dropping through a forest of pine trees, past virgin land being cleared for building plots, down to the marina. The boat brigade are hurrying to pick up fresh baguettes for breakfast, the quay is crammed with ocean-going cruisers, rarely used to go further than the next bay but in constant need of attention. The yacht club is buzzing, there's an excitement which Kendi picks up, she has a smile on her face as we hasten to the café on the harbour, nimbly leaping the bundled fishing nets hauled in overnight and now laid out, awaiting repair.

After we have finished our ensaimadas, and said *adios* to a couple of coiffed poodles reclining under the next table, there's just time to get back to the house to meet up with Ignacio who has arrived with a tape measure and his 'top man', Pepe. Pepe is muscular and bald and he and his boss are discussing which bits of the wall need to come down. They want to get a digger in, so a large chunk will have to be demolished. I am now fixated on foundations. How are they going to make sure the pool will last for ever? And while we're at it, how is he going to cope with Cedric and his broken leg? Pepe looks bemused at hearing a woman spout such nonsense.

Ignacio however makes a fist of at least considering this seriously. Yes, he will of course make sure the pool is the very best he can build but, as I will be away for a while, had I considered putting a new roof on the house because the old one doesn't look good? Pepe, Ignacio and I look to the roof for signs of its imminent collapse. 'I can give you a new super roof and have it done before you get back and then we can discuss the pool again.' *No problemas.*

Now I know why he got that psychology degree. 'All right,' I can't believe I'm hearing myself say this, 'but how much is it going to cost?'

Ignacio says he'll be back with his *presupuesta*, which is Spanish, he tells me, for an estimate for the work which we will agree before he begins. I ask if he has heard an English phrase 'sharpen your pencil'. Ignacio says certainly he has. So I said, well you'd better sharpen it then.

Impulsively giving Ignacio the go-ahead for the new roof means I have to carry all my stuff – beds, bedding, chairs, chest of drawers, the odd fat spider and a dried-up mouse Jake left behind – downstairs and cover it all with dust sheets before I leave for Greece. I can well imagine what's in store when I get back from my filming trip. It hasn't helped that on my last night under the old roof I was woken from a delicious sleep by a rumpus in the kitchen. When I staggered downstairs the old stove was rattling. Whatever was in it was impatient to be out, so I tentatively opened the door and found, sitting in the ashes, a little owl black from beak to claw. A strangled squawk was all he could muster but once I had his tiny body in my hand, the soot dusted off easily. He soon got his act together, pecking at my finger, wanting to be off.

This little fellow must be a Scops owl, tiny enough to fall headlong down a stove pipe, the same one who keeps me awake at night. I carried him out and threw him to the stars but he flew straight into the pomegranate where he tooted all night long.

Blearily next morning, in a rush to get to the airport, I just have time to grab the ladder out of the shed and discover, as I suspected, that Boris hadn't put mesh over the stove pipe in the roof, so the owl, thinking he'd found a dark hidey-hole, had taken quite a tumble. Luckily I was around to extricate him and even luckier that Ignacio, about to start on the roof, will fix the pipe. I leave a hasty note asking him to check the stove just in case my little owl doesn't wise up and takes another header down it again.

By the time I get to Luton to board the private jet taking

the Greek Royals on their secret mission to Thessaloniki I am in need of a long rest, relieved to be at last heading to the enchanting Greek islands after the Mallorquín disaster zone I've left behind.

Happily, the Greek filming trip looked as if it might be less manic. No chaos there, yet. Everything had been planned, as if in a military operation, to perfection. Our plane carrying the King, Queen Anne Marie and their five children, touched down in the northern port of Thessaloniki right on schedule but shortly afterwards, as news got out that the King was on board, Greece went bananas. Crowds arrive in their thousands to welcome the family and an angry government, outsmarted, sent emissary after emissary to try and get the King to turn back. But no, Constantine had chartered two small cruisers and was determined to plough on with us in tow.

As King Constantine wanted to make a pilgrimage to one of Greece's most holy sites before he began his adventure we sailed towards ancient Mount Athos, which sits with its monks miles away from the world. One of these monks came with a fast boat to ferry Constantine and his sons to the monastery. He hadn't washed for weeks, which probably explains why no women are ever allowed – or want – to go near.

Soon after the religious stopover we all set off again on a long sail south, agreeing to rendezvous at the Bridge of Halkiva at midnight. The Royals took the lead, steaming ahead as we chugged behind through a narrow, treacherous strait of deep water under an unbelievably starry sky. I was busily entranced with flickering lights on the far shore when suddenly our own lights went out and the engine stalled. The boat began rolling and then drifting. As the skipper tried to re-start the engine, it occurred to me that it was an awful long way to swim to safety. The water, which a moment before had seemed darkly glamorous, became, just as quickly, inky and unwelcoming, not helped by our radio link going on the blink.

Eventually, as we all shivered and shook in the cold night air, the boat carrying the Royals came back and hauled us all on board. Here we stayed for the fortnight. Our boat never got fixed so we all had to bunk down in very cramped conditions, seven Royals and a crew of five. Queen Anne Marie on her first traumatic trip back to Greece now had her privacy compromised, as morning after morning she looked across her breakfast table at a couple of baseball hats eating a full English of sausage, egg and bacon, while she endeavoured to keep up standards, sipping Earl Grey tea from a porcelain cup. She never flinched. The poor cook below deck, meanwhile, was having a tough time having to feed so many extra mouths. He came up with the brilliant idea of dishing up meatballs every meal, every day of our trip.

Whenever there was a lull in the proceedings, I'd sneak on to the usually empty upper deck for a quick kip but my cover was blown spectacularly one hot afternoon when the Greek air force came calling. I heard the roar as I lay, eyes closed on the sunbed. By the time I'd raised myself a monster was upon me, a great, thundering machine that rocked and buffeted the boat. It had apparently come to menace and signal our position to two warships gathering on the horizon. As the plane came back for a second swoop, Princess Alexia, the King's oldest daughter, poked her head up through the hatch shouting at me to lie flat. Just in time, the plane had circled and come back for more, bearing down, but this time also wiggling its wings as it made its pass. If this was weird it got weirder.

Torpedo boats then appeared, forcing us to change course, pushing us towards the shore. The sight of all this gunmetal grey in a clear blue sea was beginning to be a bit unnerving. I couldn't understand why the Greek government had to deploy its armed might to get Constantine off its back. By the time we anchored for the evening in a bay off one of the small islands, the situation was becoming bothersome. In something 007 would have relished, frogmen swam under our boat in the black of night in an attempt to cut off our radio communication.

Unfortunately, they didn't quite manage it. Next morning the ship-to-shore radio went berserk with demands from every television news channel and newspaper across the globe wanting a stake in this Greek farce. It fell to me to field the press as best I could, although it put me once again in the firing line. ITN were first with their request for an exclusive. Sorry, you had your chance. ITV were offered the story but turned it down. It didn't put ITN off or the rest of the inter-national news media, which now flew in to track us down.

It was a great gig for them, of course, commandeering helicopters and fast boats in a lovely summer to race through the tranquil Greek isles in an attempt to be first to catch Constantine before the Greek military got to him. All this meant I now had a pile of extra work to do, which in practice meant nightly news feeds to Sky in London, who had joined forces with Fox TV in America and bought up the rights to all this from a dodgy radio link on a rickety boat. My documen-tary, which I'd hoped could be carefully crafted in calm waters, had to wait as headlines and brinkmanship seized the hour.

No one won that summer. Constantine finished his cruise but the government nursed its wrath, storing enmity to use against the Royals later. All I know is that when I boarded the plane at Thessaloniki after what should have been a restful and idyllic Greek odyssey, I was mightily looking forward to being in Mallorca again.

This is the problem, I've decided. Just as I begin to think of saying my farewells to the island, something happens to ensnare me again. We've stumbled down a rock-strewn hill-side to reach the sea and find solitude, just me and Kendi. It's a long tramp to this place but after Greece all I want is to close my eyes and listen to the waves. Here I can lay out on a rock and sunbathe, diving off into the cool ocean when it gets too hot knowing no one else will disturb my swim in this isolated cove and knowing, too, a mammoth jet isn't about to belly-flop us. Moments like this make it difficult to contemplate leaving.

Kendi's funny, she's still queasy with water. She's not sure if she should bark at it to clear off or press her wet and clammy body against me in the hope I'll protect her. The sea is deep and clear and further out where rocks give way to sand all around becomes suddenly emerald, crystal and sparkly. All my expensive bikinis bought for Greece are finally being put to good use although no one except me and my dog gets to appreciate them. We stay in this place until the sun starts flaming and dropping behind the island of Dragonera, tired finally with so much swimming, but reaching the path high on the cliff again is tricky in the twilight. The boulders seem so much more slippery and a bit treacherous but with a few firm handholds and a lot of pushing Kendi uphill from behind we eventually make it to the top as darkness descends and a moon rises. It is easy now, through the pinewoods lit like this by quiet light. As Kendi and I walk the five miles back, tripping occasionally on the rocks in the road, it occurs to me we haven't seen anyone all day.

———

I had expected on my return from Greece to find my house open to the heavens but instead Ignacio has done as he promised. I have a beauty of a roof with old tiles mixed in with new and, even better, layers of insulation, protection between me and the hot night sky. At bedtime there is a huge difference, a coolness under the eaves which transforms my sleep and a sweetness knowing that all holes have been filled and there will be no more night-time visitations from inquisitive little birds or worse. The promise being realised in the house after all my effort is another ensnarement. To see an old house come alive like this is exciting. It's like an oil painting I've nearly completed, for my eyes only, to be secretly thrilled about. As long as no one comes along to ruin it.

After such a triumph with the roof, I begin to think the making of a pool might be a cinch after all. When Ignacio shows up looking pleased with himself I tell him how impressed I am with his work and ask him when we can start on the pool. He says he has given this a lot of thought and has managed to procure the very best person on the island, an expert in construction, who will build a work of art. He will bring him up to the house tomorrow.

At nine the next morning Boris's Carlos arrives on his motorbike and hangs around, lurking behind a bush on the road. I can't quite work out this odd behaviour but Ignacio soon bowls up and Carlos and he walk round to the 'back-side', the back of my house, to discuss the pool. When I join them Carlos is introduced to me as the person who is going to be in charge of the work. So this is Ignacio's so-called expert. Carlos blushes, twisting his cap between his fingers. 'Ignacio,' I whisper, as I haul him away from Carlos, 'this is the guy who built these walls that are falling down and you're telling me he's an expert?' Ignacio tells me not to worry, goes over to Carlos and the two go into a huddle.

After it's over and Carlos manages a smile, Ignacio says it's all okay, he's sorted the problem. 'What do you mean, it's okay? What did you say to him?' I feel heated.

'Oh, I asked Carlos if he was really the person who built all this crap,' gesturing with his open arms, encompassing the whole site.

'And what did he say?'

'He said Boris thought you did not want to go to all the expense so he cut back and economised on the foundations.'

I cannot find the words in Spanish to convey I'm about to go ballistic, but Ignacio is ahead of me. 'I have brought you the *presupuesto*,' he says in a mollifying voice and shoves an envelope into my fist. 'Now you've had this very bad experience,' he soothes, 'you'll want to pay for only the best.'

It takes me at least a day and a half to not go on the hunt for Boris but after telling myself I should be '*mucha calma*' over something I can't do anything about I begin bit by bit to unwind again, although this time, I promise myself, I am definitely not going to let Carlos or any of them out of my sight, when they start excavating the hole for the pool.

———

Mateo, one of the trio of old men who frequent Sancho's, is sitting in a chair in the small balcony over the village restaurant, its long green shutters thrown wide to catch whatever air there is. This must be where he lives. I'm reading a newspaper and I can see him clearly. The morning is still and already hot and here's this old man at his open window on a kitchen chair, his head cradled in his hands. Every now and then Mateo lifts himself and props his head on an arm as if it's all too exhausting. He has on a vest and is plainly distressed. It has been an unbearable night, humid and close, and as Mateo's in his eighties and obviously not too well, he must have battled to get through it. I'm not quite sure what I can do but after a while, just as I am about to see if Sancho might go over and help, the old man notices me. In an unhurried moment he lifts his hand, hardly an acknowledgement, and smiles. He stays seated at the window as I finish a coffee and wave goodbye.

Later that morning at around eleven a gathering of men huddling in small groups appears in the square, their hands in their pockets, talking quietly with one another but even so a hum sets up which becomes louder as more and more arrive. I think there has been some effort to put on best clothes. The carpenter is here with his impressive black moustache and his two sons, also in the square are the baker and the garage mechanic; all the tradespeople have gathered. In the ten minutes it takes for the church clock to strike twenty-two times every street is full. Everyone is waiting for something.

From the house with the bright red shutters, a coffin emerges followed by a line of family members. It takes them no time to enter the church or for the crowd to just as quickly process in behind.

So the dapper little man who loved his art deco house is dead. It happened, I understand, quickly and unexpectedly. He'd been pestering the local council the week before to get them to close off the side street overlooking his garden so that it might be protected from youngsters throwing rubbish. It obviously won't happen now.

Soon, the short church service is over and the crowd is out again. By a quarter to twelve it's almost as if the funeral has never happened. Everyone has gone, except for the old man. Mateo is still there, watching from the balcony.

———

Through the year the village keeps a gentle pace, its pulse only quickened by its life-enhancing fiestas. On saints' days and religious holidays and days when big fights from long past are remembered, local people lay out the bunting. I can never keep up with the fiestas in the year, although early warnings always arrive on the back of a truck. A hoist with a man in a bucket goes down each side of the main street, threading paper chains in and out of balconies and back across the road. The place is strewn, ready. A week later the party begins, music and feasts cooked in barrels split in half and filled with fire feed everyone for just a few pesetas. It all takes place in the square under the plane trees and has a set pattern. The children come first in the early evening, then as they go to bed tired and excited, the band changes gear and the grown-ups get to make a ton of noise into the early hours.

As if village folk don't have enough fiestas of their own to organise they also take on some in San Telm. In high summer, the ladies of the village deploy their skills on the harbourside where they lay on one of the most evocative banquets of the year. Held as the sun sets over Dragonera, long trestles are laid with paellas which have been bubbling on barbecues on the beach. Those lucky enough to have bagged a space on a bench on a hot night like this are in for a treat. Over paper cups of wine shared with merry strangers, this has to be one of the best.

It was during the summer fiesta season I realised I was being cased. Whenever I turned up on the island, there'd be the inevitable roar of a motorbike racing past my house at all hours and then just as quickly hurtling back. My comings and goings were watched and photos snatched. It really didn't matter who I was with or what I was doing, the inevitable photo would appear in the English newspapers in the Andratx *papeleria* a couple of days later. As regular as swallows descending in summer, the press religiously checked out my status. It got so that anything would do. Like the unremarkable photo that appeared in a national paper of me reading a book laid out on the sand. Going to the beach started to become a hazard, instinctively feeling a camera was on me and finding, later, it was. The press got brazen, once chasing me along the bay, shoving a camera in my face because they felt like it, upsetting me with their thoughtlessness. I was what they called a celebrity and in Mallorca, with no legal protection, I was therefore up for grabs. Car chases through the backstreets of Andratx, things turning nasty when cornered up dead ends, strange people listening in to conversations over dinner in restaurants, made me more protective than ever of whatever private space I could find on the island. Gunther becoming a gaucho didn't help. I met him and the local vet as I am heading off to Palma for dinner, trotting up the track towards me. He is astride a black stallion and so is the vet. At first I don't realise it was Gunther. He looks like an Argentinean horse rustler with his black cape, black hat and black boots. All he lacked is a mask and he could well be Zorro too. The horses rear at the sight of the headlights and as I edge past, the rider theatrically throws back his cape and careers off, cantering up the hill into the dusty blackness. I know then it had to be Gunther.

Gunther didn't last long as a gaucho. I don't know why. He spent a few months trekking into the mountains and then lost interest. The two horses are now free to graze wherever they wish and have ended up invading my privacy by blockading my back gate.

Every time I want to go out or come in I have to bribe them. Usually with an ensaimada. They aren't the kind of horses you take liberties with either. They're wild. They'll charge down the road, necks outstretched, teeth bared, if they see someone new on their patch. They are handy with their back legs too, lashing out with big kicks and flying manes. I can easily leap the back gate now. They've got me trained. I have to have a regular supply of ensaimadas in my pocket because without them negotiation is never an option.

As with all opportunists they're not content to barricade my gate but want into my garden as well. They're good in that they don't come on the patio to eat the flowers in my pots but they're set on polishing off my trees. Whenever I catch them out they canter over a piece of pig wire just behind my house, clearing it easily.

So I now need to raise and strengthen it. I choose a day when they're not around and spend hours hammering stakes and tying wire. The moment I finish they reappear, taking my fence in a single stride. So now I'm cursing and shouting and off they go, back through the pig wire but one of them catches his back leg and in a panic uproots my newly repaired fence. I'm now in a rugby tackle with a horse. I have a hoof under my arm trying to free it from the wire as he takes me and the fence, bucking and kicking, into next-door's olive grove. Somehow I manage to regain my balance and mercifully, just as the hoof comes round with another wallop, he breaks free and thunders up the valley.

After this encounter their manners improve. They treat me with a kind of horsey respect and allow me through the back gate even if I have forgotten their payola but their generosity doesn't extend to everyone. The horses block the way, whinnying if anyone else turns up. When Ignacio and his men arrive to start the pool I try to tell them to be on guard. I think they think I'm bonkers. Only when they've had their oranges nicked and bread thieved do they come to their own uneasy accommodation with the horses, which mainly consists of swearing ferociously at them.

The horses finally do a bunk when the JCB arrives to dig the pool and I suddenly miss their clip-clopping up and down the road, stopping to snort over my garden gate at night. It used to give me the creeps, but with these two loose on the range I never had to worry about unwelcome intruders.

While the stallions stay away Carlos makes headway. He comes and goes on his motorbike and works with wire and cement so thick nothing should shift afterwards. As I can't stay and supervise for ever I've persuaded my father, who takes an interest in these kind of things, to come and house-sit. He and Pepe get on well. When Pepe encounters my father, under a panama hat reclining on an old wicker chair watching the work progressing on the pool, he asks where is Señorita Selina. I like the Señorita bit. My father tells him, '*El Capitan, she no aqui.*' The boss, she's not here. Pepe takes a moment to consider this and comes to the reasonable conclusion my father can be trusted with 'Señorita Selina, she *loco*, no?'

———

There's a lot of activity at the house with the red shutters in the village. It has only been a few weeks since the dapper little man died but his garden has been ripped up and a skip has appeared. The builders have moved in and are lifting stuff out by the sackful. When I go and investigate, along with old doors and a pile of rubble a whole life has also been dumped. A large black-and-white photograph of a family – a mother, father and child posing in their Sunday best – has survived, its fall cushioned by a bag of sand. The photo is in an ornate oval gilt frame with a lover's knot, it must have been taken in the 1950s, and although the photo is faded, I'm certain the father in the frame is the man who has just died. Dozens more photos lie wasted in the skip along with suitcases, chairs and a painted wooden tea caddy with 'Te' written floridly across the lid, which lifts to reveal tea leaves still inside. There is a porcelain doll and a child's picture book that has pinned on each page a neatly folded linen hanky telling the story in Spanish of a roguish wolf who sneaks in to steal sheep. The wolf on the front cover of *El Lobo y las Ovejas* is wearing an emerald green shirt and yellow trousers with a bright red bandanna round his neck. He's running off with a poor little lamb in a pink spotty frock under his arm. The book I notice has hardly been touched, its pages never turned, because the hankies are still unused.

Soon the ornate garden and its vivid mosaics will be uprooted along with the fountain and the oranges and lemon trees and replaced with modern tiling. The dapper little man's daughters look as though a burden has gone.

While all this is happening José gets out of a taxi. José is one of the three old men who used to frequent Sancho's. I haven't seen him for a while and here he is, having come all the way from Palma. He tells the driver to wait and goes into the bar. Sancho, who's watching a cop show on TV, throws his arms round him, oh so pleased he's back. José is now in an old people's home in Palma, because apparently he'd been found wandering, dazed, in the village late at night. For a few minutes these two old friends talk and laugh and then José quickly says he has to go, the taxi's waiting. Sancho hurries over to his sweety jar and returns, emptying its contents into José's hands. 'Take these, take some more,' implores Sancho.

José gives Sancho his loveliest smile, thanks him for the sweets and after another hug climbs into the taxi and leaves. Sancho's lower lip begins to tremble as he starts to weep. 'You'll see him again, Sancho,' comforts someone nearby.

'No,' says Sancho, 'I will never see José again.'

nine

The Saharan wind is picking up speed, it's brought down the ripe pomegranates hanging at the top of the tree and there's a thickness to the air. I'm sheltering inside, having a rummage because the animal sanctuary needs to raise money for a new refuge and someone will be arriving shortly to collect. Isobel turns up soon, a softly spoken Scot, the last person I'd expect to see running a rescue centre. She's got on a pretty, flower-sprigged frock, her pale skin protected by a straw hat and although she's driving a chunky truck appears fragile. She is, however, brisk. She can't stay long as she has other stuff to pick up but wants to know if I'll come and meet the helpers on their bring-and-buy stall this Saturday. 'Och, do come,' she says, 'we're easy to find. Follow the signs to the Magalluf car boot.' She eyes a pair of crocodile cowboy boots I seem to have acquired from somewhere and dropped in the pile for her to sell.

'I'll definitely try,' I promise as she hurtles off stirring up the dust behind her.

Magalluf is a bit of a nightmare. The car boot is held every Saturday on the outskirts of the resort but after driving three times round the ring road I have to cave in and ask for directions in a café down a side street. A helpful waiter produces a map, turning it upside down before pointing to the place I'm supposed to be heading except I still can't quite get my bearings and my expression must give me away. Like Manuel in *Fawlty Towers*, he throws the map aside and deprecatingly, concedes, 'Señora, you know nothing – eh.'

Eventually the crowds trooping in the heat lead me to the spot. It's packed with stalls and for a moment I feel like bottling it but Kendi's spotted a docile Labrador basking in the sun and I can see the crocodile boots from here. There's a lot of activity around the stand as Isobel's team of helpers, mainly women along with an odd fellow or two who've been roped in to help lift things, do brisk business. In the melee I manage to buy a piece of blackened old wood carved with angels which looks vaguely ecclesiastical and set off to walk back to the car when one of the helpers calls after me, asking if I'll come to a meeting of the Santa Ponsa Ladies' Club the following Saturday night. As I can't think of a good excuse why not, I say I will.

By the time next Saturday comes round I'm not feeling like heading to Santa Ponsa. It means I have to put Kendi back in her kennel earlier than normal and I'm concerned because the tips of her ears are reddened and sore and she yelps if I inadvertently touch them. It will mean a trip to the vet on Monday, but I said I'd go to the do, so go I will.

Santa Ponsa is situated on the coast. It has a fine sandy beach but layer upon layer of apartments and hotels have obliterated the natural beauty of the bay. The Santa Ponsa Ladies meet at a country club on the edge of a pine forest, on the eastern outskirts of the town, a private members' affair with gyms and beauty salons, tennis and golf where they get down and dirty to cajole enough cash out of their supporters to fuel their refuge.

I manage to park my muddy four-wheeler behind a well-placed bougainvillea in the car park and ditch my dirty espadrilles for a pair of kitten heels just as the ladies arrive, carefully manoeuvring their expensive motors into the reserved members-only spaces close to the main entrance. Just inside the front door is an illuminated fountain, which drops a shimmering cascade of water over a bed of pebbles. There's Muzak piping and a marble black-and-white tiled floor which leads to a large reception room where everyone's in such full animated chirp already, clutching their pina coladas and whisky sours, no one notices me.

It means I can do a full recce of the room and decide my next move. There's a lot of white and lemon frocks and bronzed arms and legs topped off with big jewellery and strappy gold stilettos. These are high-maintenance women, nipped and tucked, all pretty formidable. I get the feeling this must be one of their regular get-togethers, an excuse to come, check on progress and chivvy each other along, because I've happily decided I'm definitely superfluous to these proceedings.

Once they've done the social niceties it's down to business. Tables have been laid for a candlelight supper and everyone hurries in to discuss what next they must do to keep their animal refuge solvent. They are a determined bunch. I find myself next to a striking woman, Rebecca, who runs a beauty parlour in Palma. She tells me the refuge was started in desperation by an English woman many years back who couldn't put up with the cruelty she saw all around her. Her mission was to take in abandoned animals, not put any healthy animal down, but to find them good homes or keep them for ever in her care. Over the years, more and more people have pitched in to help, horrified at finding the dream island they'd retired to overrun with suffering. They have managed to rescue thousands of animals, donkeys, cats, dogs and horses.

'Have you been to the refuge?' Rebecca suddenly asks. I tell her I have. She then says it's important to remember it is not just the Brits who run it. So many nationalities are in this with us, especially local people, Mallorquíns. 'Our main worry right now, however,' says Rebecca, 'is that the council in Palma is pressurising us to leave our home and we have to find another place fast. It means buying land and that, as you know, is becoming more and more expensive.'

'Why don't you tell the council you're not going to move until they find you somewhere else? I would have thought that only fair.'

Rebecca says her members don't want to make enemies of local politicians on the council as they are uncertain of what they might do to them. 'You wouldn't believe how some people loathe our sanctuary,' says Rebecca. 'We have to barricade ourselves against arson, some of our animals have been poisoned and others stolen. We go into many difficult and dangerous situations to rescue creatures and once we've got them, then we defend them, we will do anything it takes, we will never let our animals down.' By the time Rebecca has finished her tale of heroics and woe, I've decided the ladies of Santa Ponsa would do the Paras proud.

Next day, back in my shabby espadrilles, I manage to see Nico, briefly, on my way to collect Kendi. Pointing at her ears, I ask him what has happened to them because they're now bleeding. 'It's the flies,' he says. 'She gets bitten by the flies. I am putting a, how do you say it, mixture on her ears.'

I let out a long sigh. What next? 'Nico, you must let her off the chain all the time because she can't get away from the flies,' I say. 'This is very serious.'

Nico looks hurt. 'I cannot. My father has to go to Son Dureta this week,' he tells me. 'It's his breathing. We have to go in each day to see him.'

'So what is going to happen to Kendi if your father's ill? How are you going to cope?'

'Oh, I will still feed her,' he says.

'But she needs exercise, you can't tie her up all day!'

Nico shrugs.

Kendi's not interested in such matters, she's gearing herself to jump like a jack in a box at the two dogs tied up at an old farmstead further up the track. I have her on a lead as we quietly pass their place. The bigger of the two is lying with his head between his paws, dreaming, but Kendi's not having any of this, she puts on her biggest bark, shocking him out of his reverie so he leaps straight up, snarling and straining at the chain. It is all over in a moment but the sudden drama of all this can't be good for any of us. Particularly as it happens every single day.

Kendi can curl up into a little dog when she wants. It's because she's used to her tiny kennel, I guess. At my place she's bagged a favourite chair under the vine, which she tucks herself in and round, crossing her slender feet at the front so that her paws drape down loosely while she sleeps. If I'm reading she'll seek me out, tiptoeing round to shuffle up, her head gently edging on to my lap so she can make eyes at me. If I resist, it's an offered paw and ears tight back and if this love-up fails it's back to a firm nudge with a brown wet nose. She's very quick to buckle, though. A cross word and down she'll go, cowering, before rolling on to her back in submission. If I attempt to pull her up she'll yelp as if I'm about to hit her, her spirit is so timid and worn down. At these times I try not to chastise, only glad when she sometimes shows an occasional flash of wilfulness in her careering off, round and round the field peeping out from behind the bushes, not coming when I call.

She's become firm friends with a small wiry dog whose owner, Marie, a German girl, is the latest renter of Lauren's house. When the pup first clapped eyes on Kendi he was so terrified he didn't come near for a week but his inquisitiveness got the better of him and one day he shimmied through the gate when Kendi asked him in to play and soon they were into chasing one another, a wild game only ending with the two of them collapsing in near exhaustion on the terrace. Watching them play makes the thought of Kendi and what's about to befall her saddening. I can't imagine how Nico is going to manage if his father is ill. It means I am going to have to actively think of how she can be rehomed, but prising her off Nico won't be simple. She's his property and Mallorquíns don't give these things away so easily. I can't take her to Britain, no matter how much I would love to, she would have to go into quarantine for six months and that's something I cannot begin to contemplate. Perhaps Marie, who has grown fond of Kendi, might offer her a home. I sound her out. She says when I tell her Kendi's story that she would love to take Kendi back to Germany as a playmate for her pup but 'Berger Allemand', as she calls Alsatians, were Hitler's favourite dogs, and today those with far-right views often have them as pets. She feels she can't be subjected to such a stigma.

The following morning, a Monday, a team of Ignacio's men arrive early at eight to start on the walls round the swimming pool. They've come on motorbikes and old cars, hitting quite a speed over the bumps on the track. An hour later after they've all had breakfast under the old olive tree, Pepe arrives with the day's building equipment, turning the decidedly wobbly road even wobblier with the weight. I've noticed large ruts have appeared and craters too. I'm sure Gunther is not pleased. He's done his bit to keep the road passable, digging channels to take away the rain water. All this heavy use is doing serious damage.

Later that morning I'm on my way to Andratx when a little way down the track I come across a tree lying across the road, which is strange. There hasn't been a gale. I can't think where it's come from, but as I'm hauling it away, Gunther arrives. He's in full road-repair kit, his trousers clamped with string round his ankles, heavy boots and a brown handkerchief on his – so far – unsweaty brow. 'Good morning, Selina.' He's at his gap-toothed best.

'Hello, Gunther, what can I do for you?'

Gunther ambles over and helps lift the tree. 'I vant to talk about the road.'

'Yes, I guessed you might, but why did you need to block-ade it?'

'I vant to speak seriously to you about it.'

'All you have to do is ask me to stop and I will stop.'

'That is not the point,' he says. Gunther then turns his guns on Ignacio, who I sense he resents, blaming him for the damage that has been done to the track.

'Gunther, before you say any more, let me go now and get Pepe to come and speak to you. You can tell him how you want it repaired.'

Gunther seems satisfied with this suggestion. Pepe meanwhile is deep into choosing which stones he'll use for the rebuilding of the wall and so, basically, doesn't want to know. I have to insist. Gunther has blocked the road. '¿Como?'

'Yes, Gunther wants to speak to you.'

'Señorita Selina, me busy, *mucho trabajo.*'

'Yes, I know you have much work to do but Gunther has put a tree across the road and you have to come with me and speak to him.'

I enunciate all this very slowly. Pepe looks at me as though I've taken leave. Now he knows for sure I'm loco. I'm beginning to think I am too.

Pepe and I wander down to meet Gunther who immediately regales us with the right way to repair the channels, mimicking how he'd use a spade to go down deep, explaining that this is the proper way, the Mallorquín way of doing it. Pepe, being Mallorquín, folds his arms, eyes rolling. Gunther, who's got the audience he craves, wants to take us further down the track to show us where the canals should go but Pepe decides now is the time to stop this lunatic and says the best thing is to speak to his boss Ignacio about the road. At this reasonable suggestion, Gunther then does something most odd. He throws his arms up above his head and then falls to his knees in the dust, prostrating himself, kissing the ground and at Pepe's feet intones, 'Oh, Ignacio, oh, the great and magnificent Ignacio.'

Pepe's mouth drops open as someone witnessing an act of gross indecency might.

Pepe finds it hard to speak to me as we leave Gunther sprawled on the road and return to the house. I have a feeling he blames me for this uncalled-for interruption to his work, but what can I do? At least I'm not the only one round here who's nuts.

As work round the pool progresses and the walls rise again thick and strong my fury at Boris begins to dissipate. His design and eye for proportion I am forced to admit has been masterful, transforming the place with its surprising vistas and cosy, private places. So what if Boris's wall wasn't built to last, its replacement hasn't taken long to erect. Once the pool has been filled with water I'll never want to sunbathe anywhere else.

Ignacio has instructed Pepe to borrow an old water bowser and pick up several loads of fresh spring water from the mountain on the other side of the village to fill the pool. Julio, another of Ignacio's guys, is helping out. They're both in the cab of a decrepit truck with a tanker on the back, all smiles. The filling of the pool looks like it's as much their treat as it is mine so carting ten loads of water, which they think they'll need, is going to be fun. Well, it is until the fifth load runs away with them. Everything had been going smoothly. They'd made trip after trip, tipping the water straight into the pool before trundling off for more. They'd been gone too long which made me go looking and when I ran into the river of water running down the road it wasn't long before I found Julio and Pepe in a state of near desperation. Their tanker had hit one of Gunther's channels and rocked so violently it rammed into a concrete post. Things, as far as Pepe was concerned, weren't good and Gunther, if not me, was definitely to blame.

Cedric isn't having a good day either. Back at the house, limping, he is muttering about the underwater lights which won't illuminate. 'Fucking hell,' keeps erupting from the darkened pool house.

'What's the matter, Cedric?'

'Don't ask me, I'm only the fucking plumber.'

When I try placating him with how much worse it has been for Pepe and Julio today, what with all the water running away, Cedric launches forth with 'Only a bird like you,' – or words to that effect – 'could do this to a guy like me. What made you think a fucking pool was going to work with no fucking water or electricity?'

'But Cedric,' I shout back, 'remember you're the expert round here and I do have a generator.'

That evening with the pool half filled and the men finished for the day I feel I deserve a dip. It is heavenly, the warmth in the air and the fading light makes me feel I could float here for ever. I'm just coming round to believing that my perfect pool has been worth all the effort when something black swoops in and hits me. It's a bat. A big one. Then there's another and another. They're scooping up water in mid-flight, dipping and rising, jerkily, just as taken with this new attraction as I was a moment before. Now, I'm the kind of girl who likes bats, but only when I can see them, not up to my neck in water in the dark when I can't.

The christening of the pool, I rapidly decide, will have to wait until the wildlife has done its thing and as the pool gets topped up in the days ahead, other creepy-crawlies come to make its acquaintance. Exotic dragonflies zip in, so too water beetles, paddling round until they get so tired I have to fish them out. The bats get into the rhythm, allowing me to have my dip before they take theirs, usually in late afternoon. They take up residence in the tiles under the porch and hang upside down to get a grandstand view of when I'm in and when I'm not.

After the pool is finished Ignacio's men start cleaning and revealing the stones on the house that Boris said couldn't be done. This gang of men are strong and resourceful and work so hard at something they are clearly so good at that my quirky little place turns, almost overnight, into a spectacular artwork. All I need to make life lovely is electricity, which means my attention turns full-time to Ignacio, the only person who thinks it possible and the only one foolish enough to tell me so.

The next step, he says, is to put together a project, to get everyone who wants electricity in the valley to pay their share, only then can he go to the Ayuntamiento and get the right 'permissions'. I try telling him I have done my best already and failed. He isn't downhearted. No, the moment he gets everyone's signatures, he says, he will dig up the road and Gesa will definitely come and lay an electricity cable powerful enough to feed every house. It is all so simple.

Which of course it wasn't. First, as I had already discovered, not everyone wanted electricity and the ones that did made out they didn't. Then Ignacio suddenly found he had another 'project' to do for a cousin of his lower down the road and only after he'd finished this, he said, could he start on ours, but the clincher for most subscribers who were half-hearted at best, was that after ten years anyone could nab a piece of what was about to become a very expensive piece of action and not pay a cent towards it.

So, if the area is so special, I want to know, why can't we bury the ugly telephone lines and perhaps drop a water pipe in the trench while we are at it? Ignacio is horrified. Who ever heard of such a thing? It is a fact of life in Spain that one good idea shouldn't be spoiled by another. That's too much to expect. If electric has to go in, the road is ripped up and filled in. When water has to be put underground it's no problem to tear up the road again. The water company doesn't have anything to do with Gesa and neither have any truck with state-owned Telefonica.

Having established I'm in a fix I decide I need a new lawyer, someone I can speak to, a Mallorquín versed in the subterfuge and obfuscation of his fellow islanders, a man who knows how-things-work-around-here, who can, perhaps, come and hold my hand.

Don Señor José Feliu, who has a twinkle in his eye like the wolf in the picture book I'd found in the skip, sits in a glamorous office overlooking the old city walls of Palma. José Feliu is the patriarch of an established family law firm, his father and grandfather were once chief justices in an old Spain when José was young and dispatched to Britain to learn English in a solicitor's office, picking up a romantic fluency in the language thanks to a pretty girl who coaxed out the Don Juan in him.

I'm made comfy in a brown leather chair for the first of what will become many fireside chats with Snr Feliu and ask him what he thinks I should do about getting electricity. It is a tiresome subject to which I expect a weary, legal response. But no. I'm treated, instead, to a passionate soliloquy, where my worries are wrapped, my concerns shelved and the problem half-solved. He delivers, as if in a juicy whodunit, a cast of characters only he is qualified to describe and only he can fathom. In other words, I should leave everything to him, he will personally go and see Ignacio and whoever else needs seeing to sort it. I will soon have no more problems.

Soon I am skidding down the ocean freeway to the Gesa offices again, this time with José Feliu, who's not a bit enamoured with my driving, in the passenger seat. We're greeted importantly and courteously by the boss of the place, who knows José Feliu well, and there is much shrugging and gesticulating followed by another session of filling and signing of forms while José Feliu lectures me on why, as a beautiful woman, I should enjoy my life and not concern myself with these things. When I tell him it is all right for him, he lives in a house with electricity, and hasn't been threatened with his house being burned down, he says I should leave the worrying to him. This is what he is here for. Like the story of the lamb in the pink spotty dress snatched by the wily wolf who won't let go, I feel I'm in no position to argue.

Back in the village life trundles on. Whenever I see Mario on his scooter ever so slowly manoeuvring his way to work, a basket stuffed with greenery on the back, he's wearing a crash helmet. He is, I guess, setting a good example because Mario has been enlisted at the new primary school in the village to teach children all about plants. It is an inspired choice. Mario, who won't kill a weed if he can help it, is now raising and propagating plants, which means he raids everyone's gardens for cuttings and takes them to the school to show little ones how to plant, tend and grow. Some of the money collected to pay for the thanksgiving feast after the forest fire has gone towards buying young trees, which the children have planted round the school. Local people thought it a fine way of showing youngsters how much it takes for a tree to survive and what it means when a tree dies, and now one of the best gardens in the village thrives at the local primary. It seems to me, Mario has found a life here steady and sustainable and enviable. I wish I had a smidgeon of his patience and forbearance.

Instead, I am getting twitchy about rumours of development in the village which threaten its uniqueness. This village, which is almost as far as you can get from Palma, manages to fare better than most. Living here is still cosy but with the accelerated construction of new motorways on Mallorca, villages like this once lost in the country are in danger of becoming suburban, open to fast cars minutes rather than hours from the airport, no longer a beat behind the rest of the world. Soon the rock star, Annie Lennox, who has a house in the mountains, will raise her voice warning islanders to be 'very very careful' about concreting over the beauty of the place. Mikhail Gorbachev, the ex-Soviet premier, will deliver another warning when he visits the north of the island, but whenever a ban on building is declared there's a splurge of development as permits already in the pipeline get fast-tracked.

One of my favourite bits of wasteland, a magnet for seed-eating birds, is across the road from the school. It's rough and untreasured. Most locals take for granted the wildlife hiding here, but if this is ever built on there'll be no more waist-high thistles sporting the most magnificently blue flowers or prolific black figs tumbling from the tree in September, tempting small boys with their stickiness. There'll not be a shortcut through the long grass to the main road either, useful for tired little legs, perfect too for playing hide and seek. Apart from the migrating birds which stopover and feast in fields like this there are always a dozen or so resident sparrows twittering and fighting in the dust outside the school. I have to slow down in my car to avoid them and then slow again for the local boys turning up for school who shove and push each other into the road. These children have a grand life with a lot of freedom. Sometimes they troop in a long crocodile past my house, holding hands and collecting flowers, learning about Mallorca.

I wonder if the children will remember Jesus and his sheep who graze the pastures around them, a biblical scene on their doorstep, which once he packs up will be gone for ever. I can't imagine anyone continuing to follow the sheep round the valley as he does night after night, even though his solitary wanderings and sleepy moments colour everyday life, especially for the folk who wake to discover half their garden's gone.

Jesus has moved his flock to the almond groves near the old manorial ruins on the back road, away from the burned hillsides beyond my valley, which I am nevertheless still drawn to. Now the pine trees are gone high stone walls girding the hills have been revealed. Built by generations of villagers to catch earth and grow crops, they now clearly display what were once well-tended groves with an odd, massive stump of a ravaged olive tree which must be hundreds of years old. All these, once lost and hidden in the pines, have now been brutally exposed by the fire, a palimpsest of a life long past. If I touch the blackened stumps of some of these thick olives I can still feel the heat of the embers at their heart. It is sad but it is easy now to walk on ancient footpaths so starkly defined, up into the mountains without wading our way through scratchy scrub. Kendi and I always return from these walks of wonderment with filthy feet.

Even though these paths look lost they are not forgotten. Local people have acute recall of boundaries round their ancestral ruins, it is just that they choose not to visit them too often.

It is rare to find locals walking the hills although there's an interesting old man I usually see in Lorenzo's bar talking to the other old men who must walk as much as me. He doesn't smile much although there are deep creases round his very blue eyes. He is terribly thin and weather-beaten. I often come across him unexpectedly in the hills, usually sitting on a rock a little way off the path, his legs crossed, looking out towards the far horizon. Once when I was walking along the cliffs with two small boys who had come to stay he startled us. The sea crashed wildly below and there he sat, quiet and gnomish, observing us from a rock higher up. The boys responded, waving their hellos. It was the only time I ever saw him twinkle. I often thought that maybe he might like Kendi to keep him company on his long excursions into the hills but then I learned he was mourning the death of his wife and wanted solitude. I also discovered he'd once been a sea captain, which explains much.

Those who most regularly tramp the hills of the Sierra Tramuntana come from the bleak northern cities leaving mounds of stones to mark junctions, spraying dots of paint, bright blue or yellow or red on rocks to show the correct way to go. They are mainly German walkers in their middle age who arrive to enjoy the natural beauty of inland Mallorca where the sun, they hope, will shine. It is still a mystery to estate agents why Brits, on the whole, want crowded apartment blocks with sea views while Germans generally prefer more characterful homes on their own in the country. The island is certainly well mapped out, whoever is responsible.

The forest fire has, naturally and temporarily, deterred these columns of walkers who prefer less burned-out sights, so the hills which were once alive to the surprising sound of yodelling have reverted to the more entrancing song of birds enjoying a new-found perch on bare branches.

It always surprises me how a small island like Mallorca is able to add to the overall gaiety of European nations by attracting not only walkers but cyclists too, thousands of whom turn up in January and February to train on the inclines and bends of every minor road. They wear the works: Lycra, studded shoes, gloves, helmets, the lot, spreading their bright bikes three deep so that roads at this time of year are impassable. Bikers are, of course, a source of income for the roadside bars and restaurants in the off-peak months so they are always welcome.

Ravenous bikers who climb the steep hill road out of Andratx and need a refuel before tackling Puig de Galatzo find the small bar in the village of Capdella a happy pit stop and if I happen to be there having lunch it's an amusing diversion for me as well. The bar, like so many others on the island, has an unprepossessing view, but what it lacks in location it makes up in good food. Outside under a blue-and-white striped canopy amidst pots of busy lizzies and geraniums, tables are reserved which, facing south, catch the sun all day. Soon, platters of calamari grille, steak, pa amb oli and patata fritas will be dished up by a guileless young girl with a froth of brown curls. I've noticed, however, these men on their racing machines – and they are usually fellas – find it hard to prise themselves away from this convivial spot. A warm sun in late February over a cold glass of San Miguel can be, encouragingly, just a tad too tempting, even for the most dedicated.

Exercise is, in fact, becoming quite a crusade although most politicians haven't yet caught on, pumping cash instead into fast motorways, wiping out footpaths so that cars can race through tunnels but people walking can't. Such shortsightedness will come back to bite them, I'm sure, as gym membership soars and walkers, who continue to risk their lives on busy roads, rebel. It's still only relatively new but already exercise is having an impact, galvanising young and old into thinking of their health.

The fitness bug is even adding fizz to the local fiestas. The high point of summer in Port d'Andratx is the fiesta of the Virgin Mary, the patron saint of fishermen. On 17 July the port's fishing fleet decks itself in flowers and heads to sea carrying an effigy of their saint so that she might calm and pacify the water. This blessing of the sea is always performed at night, accompanied by lights, horns and music. The whole town turns out to watch Mary, draped in flowers and carried on fishermen's shoulders, process through the dark narrow streets to a packed candlelit church where the seafarers' liturgy is said. This blessing of the fishermen, usually on one of the hottest days of the year, has been going on since the fourteenth century but recently another, altogether more risqué performance, has muscled on to the quayside. The girls and boys of the local gym have taken to anchoring their exercise bikes to a stage specially erected in the open air where they rev up the fiesta, showing off their energy and biceps to an audience of mainly old ladies and young children.

As the rock music begins, the dozen or so enthusiasts, decked out in tight gym gear, straddle bikes on either side of their leader, alert to his imminent command and their cue. Children are waiting, bobbing to the beat, old ladies behind hand-held fans are tittering but when the order to go is given the troupe blast into action and everyone's riveted. The pedalling is compelling, every movement hit in synch with the backing track. Suddenly the perspiring legs of the girls and boys on the bikes start whizzing round faster and faster until the teacher thrusts his fist in the air and belts out 'Arriba', whereupon a dozen muscular bums lift up and head heavenward, where they gyrate furiously and rhythmically for a minute or so until ordered to descend so the gig can begin again. The old ladies are by now beside themselves.

A House in the High Hills

I bet it's this hunky gym teacher who's given Paco's girl-friend the oomph to take up jogging. Paco's girl is a cook, not the kind of person I'd ever imagine running. Her slow gait as she walks to the bar in a morning, smoking a fag, has never marked her out as athlete material so when I noticed her togged up in pumps and a track suit I thought it was only for effect until I overtook her in my car running along the road to the Port one early morning at around six. I am most impressed.

The elegant wife of the local electrician, who must be in her seventies, has also taken up swimming and each day does several laps in Andratx swimming pool before returning to her housework. Ignacio too has joined in, although I notice some Sundays are reserved for an altogether more sedate activity.

He meets up with his old schoolfriends in Lorenzo's bar, because Lorenzo and the guys in their trilby hats make up the local bowling club, which seems to me to be an excuse to back-slap, shout at one another and smoke cigars. Beatriz is left in charge as the boys troop off to do a bit of male bonding and compete in village tournaments but come Monday, it's back on the treadmill, the trilby's been ditched and Ignacio slips into something altogether more comfortable: his tight running shorts.

Since finding my house in the valley I hardly have a moment to think of things like gyms. If I am not walking the hills with Kendi I'm hacking back the abundant foliage that two springs in a Mediterranean year shower down. The wisteria puts on so much growth I have to unwind it from the telephone wire slung between the posts up the road, and carefully cut it free, although one year I misjudged and everyone got disconnected. The wisteria's whippy shoots are piled in the middle of the field ready for the big bonfire in the wet season, along with prunings from the almond trees and olive branches which in a couple of seasons can grow as thick as a man's arm. Since the plum tree died, a wild olive which was once so insignificant on the terrace has gone berserk in its new-found space. Soon I'll have to get a saw to one of its branches banging against my bedroom window.

The joy of experiencing lavender stuffed with bees and freesias scenting the morning air occasionally leads me astray and into serious digging, excavating holes to take important plants like a lemon tree or bay, which then have to be watched and watered. I had become passionate about jacaranda trees after my filming trip in Seville and spent days tracking down some semi-mature ones in a garden centre in the middle of the island. They arrived on the back of a truck and now cascade their lilac blue petals over my land, although they took some nurturing in their early years.

My plan to leave everything wild, to enjoy the growing green shoots after a parched summer and the abundance of wild flowers which turn up almost while I'm not looking takes great restraint, especially when there are so many tempting wonderful plants to procure. I love my bank of plumbago, for example, which froths powder-blue flowers over all my walls. I planted cuttings by the dozen and watered and weeded until now they're rampant – unlike the delicate white trumpets of the brugmansia with their bewitching night-time scent, plumbago doesn't demand too many cooling drinks on a regular basis. The brugmansia, however, like the jasmine falling over and around it perfumes every room of the house. I can forgive these delicate plants anything.

Perhaps the flower of most delight to me is the tender bee orchid, which flourishes in the tussocky grass on the hillside. To arrive from a cold damp England and find these inquisitive flowers, in such unpromising terrain, sunning themselves in the same familiar place is uplifting. It is hard not to stop and consider these fragile flowers surviving and thriving, when back in the UK they're so rare and threatened now.

This blossoming of the year casts a potent spell with its explosion of colour and variety as spring turns to summer then into spring again but like the little bee orchid I can't hang around too long. Another break away is imminent and this time it will be for longer.

I have, on impulse again, bought a farm in North Yorkshire which needs tons of loving care, but casting a deep shadow over my going is Kendi and her predicament. I cannot abandon her now and yet I don't know how I am going to cope. At least I don't have to do something immediately, there is still time.

ten

The pungency of wood smoke hangs in the valley on this clear and lovely day in early November. I've been away in the States and my first thought is to find Kendi and buy fresh fruit, bread and other provisions, although I reckon it might be best to collect what I need in the village first and pick Kendi up on the way back. It will mean a detour, following the longer track up behind the village to avoid her seeing me.

The track forks halfway, at the house where Ramon, Ignacio's cousin, lives. Ramon's house has roses round the door and peach and apricot trees in the garden. Small ripe apricots, dewy and luscious, and pulled straight from the tree are divine and Ramon, knowing this, runs out and pours great handfuls into my basket when I pass by. I like Ramon because he is effusive. He looks a little like his cousin with dark lively eyes and is always getting into scrapes with pretty women. When he's in love his orchard is tidy and well watered, but when there's a blip everything becomes as unshaven as him. Car wrecks appear, washing on the line turns grey after weeks flapping there and the long grass overreaches itself. When things get really bad, his mates from the village come and do a big sweep up, hacking back the weeds, tilling the earth, making his des res desirable again so that another glamorous female, like a migrating bird, will hopefully swoop in and sweep him up.

Perhaps his luck with women has something to do with the fact that he, like me, has no electricity. There are not many high-maintenance girls prepared to go without hair dryers or washing machines or irons no matter how sexy or romantic the man. I guess Ramon and his friends must have figured this out, which is why Ignacio is prepared to dig up the road to get his lovelorn cousin powered up, first. Ramon is always telling me he's 'looking out for me' and if he gets electricity he'll 'make certain' I get it too. Which of course makes me like him all the more even though I know it's bunkum. Ramon is not at home today so I can't ask if he has any news of electricity or when it will arrive. Which is perhaps just as well. I'm getting so that this Mallorquín way of showing a girl a good time – fibbing outrageously – is wearing thin.

It is while I'm contemplating the improbability of ever having electric light if I have to wait for Ignacio, that I think I hear Kendi yelping. It is definitely her. Her cries are carrying clearly on the air so I have to hurry, all the time wondering what on earth can have happened. As I get close I can see Kendi crouched in the dust, wincing as an angry Nico stands astride her, ready to whack her again. 'No, don't!' I manage to shout.

He spins round, surprised I'm here. 'She has been bad,' he tries to explain. 'She kill my chicken which has babies.'

The hen is laid out at his feet, dead, from a bite to its neck, its tiny chicks scudding around. Oh dear. 'She's a dog and she can't help it,' is all I can muster.

Nico shakes his head. 'My father he won't be happy. I let her off her chain for you and she does this. She no be trusted.'

Now is not the time, I know, to explain to Nico why a dog with her energy should never be cooped up. She's been used to coming on long walks with me, but while I have been away she's obviously had no exercise. As Nico hitches Kendi, roughly, back on to the chain, I tell him I understand why he is upset and hope his father won't be too cross. I can sense it's best not to ask if Kendi can come with me. Better not push it and hope he cools down. I am determined not to leave until I know Kendi will be okay and soon Nico does turn sunny although the day for me has suddenly become dull.

By evening I've decided what's to happen. I'm going to ask Nico if I can buy Kendi from him, although I know if he sells her, he'll find another dog to tie up, another poor animal with which to torment me, but at least, I tell myself, Kendi will get a second chance. While I have been away I have steeled myself to accept that Kendi has to be found a new home on the island, no matter what. I cannot take her with me, the journey is too fraught.

'*Hola*, Selina.' In the half-light at the end of the day Nico is calling. He has Kendi on a rope. Why he has negotiated the difficult track just as darkness falls, I can't fathom but Nico wastes no time. He walks in and proffers Kendi. 'If you want her, you can have her,' he says firmly.

'But why?' This is something I hadn't foreseen.

'My father has to go into hospital again and I give you Kendi. She will guard the house.'

'Oh, thanks,' is all I can say.

Nico's brown eyes start to glisten and it strikes me in spite of all that has happened, he is fond of her. 'But she's yours, are you sure?'

'*Sí*,' he says, 'she better with you.'

He turns to go, leaving me, oddly deflated, with Kendi.

She's sitting on the kitchen floor, head on one side, looking at me as if to say 'so what now?' Do I feed her and if so, on what, and where is she going to sleep tonight? None of this has troubled me before. I've always made sure Kendi got back to her kennel at night and although I've slipped her treats I've been careful not to upset her tummy with food she's not used to. Now she's apparently mine, which I still somehow can't believe, I'm going to have to think of what to do with her. A momentary panic sets in. Who is going to take her and look after her? How on earth am I going to find her a good home? Somehow I manage to obliterate my worries and concentrate on more immediate things like finding somewhere for her to kip down. The implications of Nico's impulsiveness can be dealt with in the morning.

My sitting room has a huge sofa covered in broad cream and grey striped linen with massive feather-down cushions that fills half the room. It's heaven to collapse in and the room in all its sumptuousness has been out of bounds to Kendi in all the time we've known one another. Tonight, however, as it looks like she's here for good and as I have some writing to do and I can't very well banish her, I've invited her in as long as she's on her best behaviour.

Lying carefully on the floor, she places her head between her paws, positioning herself perfectly. Her limpid eyes fix on me and she begins to whine. She's not housetrained. I wonder if she needs to go out. Moths flutter in as I prise open the heavy front door but Kendi's not for budging. No matter how much I cajole and encourage she's decided she's staying put. So here's a new revelation, Kendi hates the night, which means I'll have to accompany her. Out in the blackness my eyes take a while to adjust but when I finally manage to focus, Kendi's disappeared. The next time I look she is lying, head deep in the cushions, on my sofa, eyes closed, her feet in the air.

Bedtime is another eye-opener. The stairs leading up to my bedroom curve from the old entrance hall, and without light can be tricky. Kendi soon gets the hang of them, however. I find an old blanket and lay it outside my bedroom door so she can feel safe, close to me. She doesn't object and is there early next morning, stretching and wagging her tail. I'm not quite sure whether she thinks she's protecting me or me her. Either way this sleeping outside my bedroom on the landing floor is I think a good solution until I discover a few days later she's never spent a single night on the tiles but is instead kipping down on the sofa, creeping upstairs early when she hears me stir.

If she's crafty she is, however, clean. Each morning I expect to find a puddle or worse but she doesn't let me down. For a dog who's been reared in a kennel in a field this is amazing. In any case I walk her as soon as the sun comes up and the dew soaks my shoes as we sludge through the long grass. She hurls herself to the top of the field and waits for me to open the gate, then she'll run on again and round, doing a loop, loping back as quickly, to heel. Kendi has a way of concentrating on my feet, like a wolf circling its prey, which makes her look more ferocious than she is. I guess this is part of being a good-looking Alsatian.

These early morning walks are special mainly because the weather is often benign as the year heads towards its end. It also means we can stop and make new friends along the way. Kendi is very taken with a small hairy dog who ventures out the same time as us each morning bringing along a cheery, round-faced man who strides along on a couple of walking poles. We usually bump into one another under the holm oak marking the divergence of the paths and after a chorus of *holas* and *hasta luegas* go our different ways. Kendi likes small dogs. She doesn't feel threatened and is always happy to wag her tail at this particular bit of scruff.

Along with Kendi has come her vaccination record, an important-looking document, bound in green with a gold and red Reino d'Espana stamped on its cover. It was given to me with much solemnity by Nico a couple of days after he'd handed her over. It records the number of anti-rabies injections she has had over these last few years and I guess will come in very useful for whoever ends up with Kendi. I am trying not to dwell on our parting but, soon, I must push myself into approaching anyone with any inclination to offer her a home. Nico's lucky, he seems to have got over his anguish at saying goodbye to his dog. I suppose he has other more important matters to worry about.

His father is now in Son Dureta and Nico has to visit regularly because of his 'pulmo' problems. His lung complaint. I think it's cancer. Kendi, whenever she sees Nico, still gives him a huge welcome but has now, thankfully, settled away from him, as well she might with all the walks and fine food I am giving her. Her coat, once so harsh and dry, is now silky and with her blossoming I'm finally ready to visit the vet for a thorough check.

Port d'Andratx is busy with trucks unloading provisions and cleaners on ladders washing windows as Kendi and I fall out of the car outside Petra's surgery. I can't believe how good Kendi is, walking to heel, following my lead, being so well behaved that going to the vet's feels somehow less fraught. The feral cats are growling over their breakfast trays on the street as usual as we wade through and into reception, setting off the tinny chimes over the front door, to wait in a fug of antiseptic for Petra who has just finished operating and is in a back room, stacking cages with bandaged and knocked-out cats and dogs awaiting their owners.

There are a couple of other casualties before us in the queue. A fluffy, bad-tempered cat with her doting owner and a tearful English girl who's found four adorable puppies with floppy ears dumped in a rubbish bin near her holiday villa and doesn't know where to turn. She has them in a cardboard box, their appealing eyes and wet noses peeping over the side. Someone suggested the girl bring them here but soon Petra is spelling out the harsh facts of life. If she takes the pups to the municipal pound they'll be killed and incinerated in two weeks because no one wants them, five thousand a year are destroyed like this. The only other suggestion Petra has, trying to console the girl, is that she takes them to an animal rescue which has been set up in Calvia a few miles away. She doesn't want to distress her any more but I know, as does Petra, that this sanctuary, like so many others, is overflowing with strays. A German woman started it, hoping to save the lives of animals locked up in the council's dog pound. This council, Calvia, one of the richest in Spain, whose massive revenue is generated from visitors, seems to have hardly a conscience when it comes to wiping its streets of strays.

The girl with the pups trudges away to waste a day trying to find an unhappy solution and Kendi and I get to see Petra. I had hoped to ask Petra, amongst other things, if she might know of someone who could give Kendi a home but the box of pups has left me dejected.

Petra says what a lovely dog she is as she runs her hands along Kendi's tummy and haunches and lifts her, gently, on to the scales to weigh her but when she touches her ears, Kendi squeals, so now she has to have a blood test because mosquitoes can transmit disease and Kendi may have to have her ears amputated. I have to lean against Petra's desk to absorb this new piece of information. Surely not? Only when the test comes back, Petra tells me, can she decide what treatment to give her. Her ears are very sore, she has had a lot of flesh eaten away by the flies. To depress me even more she then says Kendi will need a ton of injections including an anti-rabies shot and have to be checked with more blood tests at regular intervals if she's going to have a pet passport. 'I haven't thought about taking her back to Britain,' I say weakly.

'Well, what are you going to do with her?' asks Petra.

Out on the street, the cats have sloped off along with the vans and the cleaners. Visitors and locals are out shopping in the sun, unhurried, taking time to talk to one another and exchange gossip about the goings-on of the district. From the restaurants there's much chattering and laying of tables as Kendi and I find a berth in a café on the quayside to discuss where we're to begin to find somewhere nice for her to live.

There is so much energy in the port, piles of swish new homes going up, there surely must be someone here who could care for her. I know she doesn't have much kerb appeal with her wolverine looks and scruffy coat and although I love her I can see she's not to everyone's taste. Perhaps if I parade her someone might take a fancy to her. You never know.

Just as I've anchored Kendi, tying her lead to a chair leg, telling her to be good, a black-and-white spotty dog pees on a menu board across the road. Kendi is not pleased. The café whose board it is, is getting a reputation for serving good food even if the chef is a bit dictatorial towards his customers. I hope he'll make an appearance soon and tell the dog to clear off because Kendi's howl has gone up an octave and is beginning to unsettle the well-heeled customers at the adjoining table.

I try ignoring her as the conversation at the next table gets louder. They're discussing their disappointment in the local fish they'd had for dinner last night. I know what they mean. Fish caught in a warm Mediterranean Sea, even if presented beautifully with too much garlic in Mallorquín restaurants, is not the same as newly landed haddock caught in the cold waters of the North Sea. They're on to the subject of *bacalao* now, dried salted cod from Iceland sold in the markets of the island and steeped overnight in water, which they say is interesting. Not as interesting to Kendi, however, as the dog across the road, who is now loitering with intent. Kendi drops, ready to pounce. Too late, she's off with the chair through the tables, across the road up the hill, and after the hound. She does let me down sometimes.

Once I've retrieved the chair, Kendi and I hoof it up the hill away from the quay, to cool off. She knows she's blown it but I'm not cross for long, this place needs a bit of a jolt.

On our way home we pass the old cinema, which is now, I notice, a classy wine store. There are new top-end boutiques selling designer gear along with beauty therapists touting cosmetic surgery, all for a wealthy and mainly German clientele, it seems. Curvy iron street lamps and colourwash is displacing the drabness of new-build much to the consternation of the older locals who still park their small boats and bait their lines amidst the shops of azures and lavenders, oxblood and buttermilks along the sea front.

Only the Café Samoa, as an odd bookend to a particularly racy collection of new cafés on the outskirts of the port, still sits as a beacon of simple fare. Its owner, a chirpy and friendly Mallorquín, has been dishing up egg and chips and cheese toasties from dawn to dusk for years now to his mainly English clients, welcoming them as though they are family. John Noakes, who Shep the sheepdog once made famous when they worked together on BBC's *Blue Peter*, is having coffee there with friends. I am so tempted, but no, I can't barge in and ask him if he fancies another dog, that would be too cheeky. In any case he has the look of someone who doesn't want disturbing, but I'm not ruling him out for Kendi either.

Ramon is galloping up the track in a state as Kendi and I march back into the village. He's leaning out of his van shouting something about how the trench will soon be dug for electricity. He's certainly very merry. I can't say I'm thrilled for his good fortune but congratulate him and walk over to Emmy Lou's to see if she has anything to add to this new development as she's been in charge of negotiations with Ignacio in my absence.

Emmy Lou is busy cooking for her Thanksgiving party because feeding the five thousand is her thing. Cars will arrive through the day, children run round the hills, and then they'll eat and drink and make music into the early hours. Bob Dylan covers are a great favourite. Emmy Lou is a good cook, able to creatively put together a banquet out of the simplest ingredients, and this year's Thanksgiving looks set to be like all the rest.

Emmy Lou has a pile of endive on a chopping board, which she's tossing into a wooden salad bowl when I arrive. Soon she's confiding that she's been talking to a newish neighbour called Heinrich who has come to live in a house on the other side of the hill. She's discovered he wants electricity as badly as us and he's getting mad that he's not down to get it when Ramon does, as he lives only a couple of hundred metres away. Emmy Lou says she thinks we should go and talk to him and then fills me in on how Jesus the shepherd has fallen out with Heinrich over a footpath on Heinrich's land. Apparently Jesus uses the footpath to take his sheep up the valley but Heinrich has commandeered the path and fenced it off, preventing Jesus and other locals using it.

It has naturally caused an enormous rumpus, stoking the general suspicion round here about foreigners who fence and wall off their property so that no one can see in. Looking into a neighbour's field is an essential part of village life. What use is a walk if you can't nose around? How can you know anything about anyone if you haven't seen it with your own eyes?

Anyway, Emmy Lou has decided we should make an effort to see Heinrich before work begins on the road so we troop down the hill and round to Heinrich who is sitting in his walled enclosure with a bottle of plonk. Heinrich is in his fifties, portly, has something to do with marketing in Palma and is soon regaling us with how the local 'mafia' have ganged up against him. I presume, by this, he means Ignacio and Ramon. He is a bit bombastic and certainly angry and keeps threatening much malice upon Ignacio if the road is dug up and he, Heinrich, doesn't get the electricity supply he wants.

It is all a bit robust for my taste but we're stuck. As the moon rises, Emmy Lou lights up and settles in for an evening chewing over tactics with Heinrich while the bottle lasts. When we finally make our exit an *entente cordiale* appears to have been agreed, which means Heinrich has decided he is going to put the boot in while we sit back and watch the fireworks.

Kendi is hiding behind the shutters when I get back. I know she doesn't like the dark and when she's frightened she's now begun to crow like a cockerel. Strange this, but she does 'cock a doodle doo' to perfection. It must be the hen run in her upbringing which sparks off her versatility because she does a 'doodle doo' first thing in the morning and all through the day and night whenever the occasion demands, rising to the challenge most infuriatingly when the phone rings and I'm answering it. Sometimes I feel sad that this lonely dog's only role model in life has been a cockbird.

The good news is her blood test has come back and it's fine. There is no hideous disease lurking in her ears but I've decided to go through with the expensive procedure of getting her a passport. I keep telling myself if she has an EU document it will help sell her to a prospective owner, it shows she's kosher, a fully paid-up member of the international doggy brigade, but in reality I guess I'm just hedging my bets because the truth is, I've already set my sights on Gunther. I've decided he is the one who should have Kendi.

It is hard to admit but I am beginning to appreciate Gunther's finer points. Used to working in television, an industry stuffed with so much insincerity and effusiveness, Gunther's candour has taken a little getting used to. I just wish he had a bigger stage on which to display his talent for reinvention and his many and varied dramatis personae.

I also have a feeling he's up to something again but I haven't yet figured out what. I've noticed car headlights wobbling along the track at about five in the morning, illuminating, raggedly, the high hills all round, and a grumpy Gunther complaining about the noise of generators in the warmth of an afternoon. He's obviously heavily into his siesta but why, I haven't yet been able to fathom.

It is a quiet afternoon when Kendi and I pluck up the energy to go visit Gunther. At the entrance to his farm an iron bedstead tied to a wooden post with a lump of twine is hanging open which means Gunther's in and doesn't mind visitors. Which isn't the same thing as welcoming them. The lumpy track leads down a hill, passing Gunther's thriving cannabis plants, before ending up right on his back doorstep.

Latin music wafts from within and there's some thumping going on but I can't yet see Gunther. He is, however, in there somewhere.

'*Hola*, Gunther,' I bellow through the kitchen door.

The music stops and shortly, heading towards me in the cool gloom, is what looks like a bad-tempered satyr. It's Gunther, a skimpy shirt open to his tummy, held in by a pair of footless tights. He's wearing ballet pumps.

'What on earth are you up to, Gunther?' I ask.

'I am dancing,' he says.

From round the corner Francine pokes her head, similarly kitted out in a floral skirt. I feel as though I've hit a bad patch of private grief. 'I'm sorry,' I offer, 'I thought I might be able to talk to you about Kendi.'

'Vy?' demands Gunther.

'Well, I was wondering, as you are an animal lover, whether you would like to have Kendi come live with you?'

The moment the words fall out I know by the look on Gunther's face, it's not going to happen. Francine, seeing my difficulty, tries translating. If we take the dog, she tells me, it will run off back down the valley to Nico again. 'I'm sorry,' she says.

I want to say Kendi won't run away and hasn't in all the time she's been with me but by now I know it's useless because they don't want this dog. I am deflated. Gunther was my last hope. Kendi's puzzled too. She's by my side, looking at him, her ears in knots.

'What kind of dancing are you doing?' I try being polite, changing the subject in case I crumble.

'The tango,' declares Gunther. 'Soon I go to Argentina to take lessons from a master so I can come back and do exhibitions round the island.'

'Really?' I begin to rally.

The tango is arrogant, fiery and demanding, a dance of the night. Kendi's used to more refined activities, preferably during daylight hours. I don't think she'd be at all keen on coming to live here permanently. There is nothing more I want to say or Gunther needs to add so I say how sorry I am to disturb them and Kendi and I sidle off. I couldn't put you through that, I reassure her as we skip along home.

It is not long after my encounter with the dancer in Gunther the gaucho, I run into Boris coming out of the bank who excitedly tells me he has leased some old sheds on the outskirts of Andratx which he intends to turn into an art gallery where he can sell his paintings and start a cultural centre. 'You'll be able to get Gunther to come and do the tango for you,' I suggest helpfully. 'He's into exhibitions.'

'That is not funny,' says Boris.

'Oh, I don't know,' I tease, 'Gunther's get-up doesn't

leave much to the imagination. It's very sexy. You'll pull in the crowds.'

For a moment Boris considers his erstwhile friend as a hot Latino lover but then spits, 'Oh, I hate him to his guts.'

A couple of days after Emmy Lou's Thanksgiving party a lightning storm slices through the island and rivers run along streets and through fields. A waterfall pours over a stone boundary wall which has never seen such water in its life and the ducks and geese in Nico's compound think they've gone to heaven. The rain doesn't let up for two days, soaking into the earth, muddying the roads and just as it begins to dry, Ignacio's digger rolls up the road to gouge out a trench for electricity. Two metres down it claws through sodden soil and rock, pulling up bucketloads of gunge to get a clear run at Ramon's and then work stops and nothing happens for ages because Gesa hasn't turned up with the electric cable. Everyone with homes beyond the devastation, which means includes me, has to leave cars and bikes and walk. Health and Safety would have a fit if they saw this deep slippery chasm. It is no place for a night-time stroll.

Despite our imploring Ignacio insists he cannot carry the trench on a bit further while the digger's here because he doesn't have permission from the council yet, so Heinrich hires his own JCB from Palma and in a day digs up the road from his house to Ramon's and links the two trenches. Now the whole stretch of track is impassable. Ignacio explodes, threatening retaliation, which pleases Heinrich no end. Heinrich then buys a cable from Gesa which he lays in his trench and insists Ignacio connect up to his. There's now a standoff. Ignacio says he can't and won't. Heinrich says you will. For some reason Heinrich wins.

Once the cable is safely embedded all along the road from the football pitch via Ramon and up to Heinrich and the road infilled and made good, Ignacio then gets permission to dig it up again so he can fulfil his promise to bring electricity to us. His JCB gets to work once more, scouring out rock making sparks fly, and we go through the whole performance again. Mud and delays and angst but what joy when finally I can switch on a light without first engaging with a generator. The two handsome electrician brothers from the village fix the wiring in the house, moving in with a mound of coloured wires and connections and leaving behind a new fridge, cooker, dishwasher and hair dryer. Bliss.

Our switch-on means Ignacio can get his own back on Heinrich because Heinrich makes the mistake of trying it on again. He slaps in a demand for us to pay him to connect to 'his' electric cable. Ignacio feels this is so bad he has to deliver the news to me personally. I commiserate as he goes through the whole sorry saga of who said what because this is Ignacio's big moment. He has on a cerise cashmere sweater and smells even more expensive. Did I know, he leans in, conspiratorially, local people prefer you, the English?

I say, 'No, I didn't, but, well, that's nice.'

'Not people like our friend.' I presume, by this, he means Heinrich. Ignacio then says Heinrich wants '*mucho dinero*' from me.

'But why?'

'Leave it to me,' he says grandly.

I don't know what Ignacio says or does but not long afterwards word gets round that Heinrich has sold up and shoved off leaving us all with hard-won harmony in our illuminated valley.

Heinrich's going coincides with the arrival of some new Germans in the village who have come independently and couldn't be friendlier. They're both, interestingly, chefs and so the village has two more eating places which means the pretty restaurant which is always busy opposite the church has competition. Dietrich from Hamburg has staked everything on the lease of the old grocery shop near Lorenzo's bar while Detmar from the former Communist East wants to barbecue ribs in the back garden of a grand house he's bought higher up the street. It's an exciting time as everyone rushes to book tables, checking in so that they can be one of the first to pass judgement on this unexpected culinary boom.

Dietrich is by far the finer cook of the two, inventive and talented, using simple fresh fare from the countryside to wow his clients. He and his wife Ingrid soon turn the grubby little shop into a cosy and imaginative restaurant with soft lights and delicious food. Detmar further up the village is altogether more commercial. He's cheaper for starters and has decided that a charcoal fire with a straightforward and unchanging menu will pull in the kind of customers he's looking for. Tables in the garden are soon booked up although he's run into a spot of neighbour trouble. The angry parrot in a cage in the next-door garden is so fed up with the invasion of noisy folk, not to mention the smell and the smoke, he's set up a particularly unsavoury and loud squawk in retaliation. Which does nothing to enhance the ambience.

The restaurant opposite the church, meanwhile, has at least one happy and content customer. A black-and-white kitten found dodging traffic in the square now kips down in a cardboard box under the large, red hibiscus in a big pot by the front door, having taken enthusiastically to living à la carte.

Which is all very lavish compared to the food my bunch of Siamese cats are being given across the street. The nearest they get to haute cuisine is an occasional lump of cheese, preferably mahon from the island of Minorca, which is stronger than the local variety. One of the kittens goes crazy for it, reaching up to place her paw in mine in the hope I might relent and give her more.

All five Siamese now share their lives with a grey striped young tom who arrived dejectedly one afternoon at teatime. He has a squint and was not in great shape so I took him to be neutered and wormed and now he's a loving and affectionate cat, who appreciates home comforts too. He also has a blanket in a box but daren't move far in case an interloper pops in and nicks it. The Siamese tolerate him but somehow, because he is alone, he looks forlorn. He also has a cough. All the cats here have coughs. I've called him Jim.

Jim knows my moods and when I'm happy he is, purring and pirouetting. When I'm feeling a bit low, he leans against me and sometimes follows me along the road to make sure I'm going to be okay which is why, in spite of his squint, I'm very fond of him. I had no idea cats like Jim fell in love until Abulita came along.

Abulita is brown and black and dainty and she's much older than him. She must be getting on for fourteen. She was once the pet of an old lady who lived in a house down the road but because of her sudden ill health was sent off to Palma and put into a home. The old lady's house with all her antique furniture and lace curtaining was sold, but the person who bought it didn't spare a thought for her cat, and she ended up fighting for survival in the village. The first I knew of Abulita was a plaintive meowing on top of the dust-bin at the road end. She was hungry, and had had at least two litters of kittens since fending for herself; the first litter had all been run over. She kept dashing from the house to the dustbin looking for food and what remained of her kittens. It was all too much for an old girl with only a few teeth left. She was easy to catch and handle and soon, she too was neutered and nursed back to health and sleekness in the garden with the Siamese. All her kittens, by then, had died, but Jim was still around.

I don't know whether she thinks Jim's one of her long-lost kittens, but he's in no doubt about her. He adores her. Wherever she goes, he goes. She licks him, cleans him and he sits there and lets her. They eat together, sleep in the same box together, their limbs wrapped round one another. He is her toy boy and now that Abulita has found a home she, like Jim, stays put. I have, or rather Pepita now has, seven cats to care for.

I would like to hug Pepita for her steadfastness in feeding the cats when she has so much to do in her own life. Her youngest daughter Pia is having a baby. It will be Pepita's first grandchild and the whole family is looking forward, excitedly, to the birth. Pia helps in the bar in the morning, getting up at five to open for the labourers arriving for breakfast at six. Bocadillos are a favourite, toasted baguettes with a thick slice of jamón serrano with pickled capers on the side. Beer and cinto tres, the local brandy, are consumed this early. No wonder everyone warms to Pia and looks forward to her unaffected welcome. From the moment she pulls back the shutters there's a cheerfulness about the place.

Francine too has turned warm. Maybe it's because I'm proving hard to dislodge but she is now offering help. Her earlier threats to smoke me out have been forgotten and she is suggesting she speak to Nico about taking care of Kendi while I am away so that, in effect, Kendi will be in quarantine with Nico on and off for six months. I will pay for her food but she will be in familiar surroundings until, Francine says, I can take her with me to the UK.

I'm not going to enlighten her by telling her I have no intention of taking Kendi with me, but her offer coming at just the right moment eases the strain. 'Do you think Nico will agree?' I ask. Francine is certain he will, particularly if I provide for Kendi. 'Will you keep an eye on her for me while I'm away?' She says she will and I am grateful. Francine's olive branch is especially welcome as I reckon six months will give me enough leeway to renew my efforts to rehome Kendi.

I can't imagine Kendi ever living in Britain, she loves the sun so much, but it's mainly because I can't actively think how I'd ever manage to get her there. Contemplating Kendi in a crate, being loaded into the hold of a plane, makes me miserable. She's nervous under normal circumstances. Fireworks upset her and whenever a gun goes off she whines and shivers, tucking up against me, trying to get into any dark cupboard so she can hide. I also know she witnessed her little brother being shot by Nico's father when he wouldn't stop chasing chickens, so how she'll cope with jet engines I can't imagine. I've already spoken to Petra and been told tranquillisers can't be given to animals on planes so the question of taking Kendi to the UK is, for me, totally out of the question.

A desultory collection of letters making up the word 'Bon Nadal' has been slung across the village street, the first indication anyone gets here that it is Christmas. With the decision taken about Kendi I'm going to try and enjoy these festive days and, like the locals, contemplate the year's end leisurely with none of the freneticism of a Britain in full gallop round the shops.

Christmas is more a church event than anything. Which is how it should be, of course, but things start hotting up the moment the old year becomes new, at midnight, when twelve bells strike the hour and twelve grapes are swallowed for luck accompanied of course by loud firecrackers exploding in the night sky over the port.

Like Northern Europe, it gets dark very early here in the Mediterranean, which makes the arrival of the Three Kings in their boat at San Telm on the evening of the fifth of January all the more eye-poppingly dramatic.

By the light of a winter moon, across a black rippling sea, Los Tres Reynos are guided to shore laden with gifts for children. Baltazar is black and turbanned, shining with embroidered gold and purple robes which flow behind him as he strides across the pebbled beach, followed by Melchior with his long white hair and a white beard and Gaspar with his green jewels and gold cloak. They mount glistening black horses, feathered and plumed, prancing in anticipation at the fast ride, cantering over the hill into the village, showering sweeties on children lining the route before giving out gifts to each one of them in the Square which will be opened the following morning. The carnival of the three kings is only the beginning. The year will be packed with fiestas kept fresh and exciting by the energy and innocence of local people, helped of course by the blessings bestowed by the weather.

If the nights in January are dark and long the days are exquisite, protecting a secret only a few are let into. Britain may be shivering and grey but here the sun can be stolen in peace for almost a month. It is always hard to return to the UK at the start of the year but I have to be back in Britain before the month is out to sign papers for the farm. This means Kendi will be left to lodge with Nico in the cooler months and only for a short time so I'm beginning to feel fairly relaxed about it.

———

It's 17 January, only a week to go before I leave, and the feast of San Antonío, the patron saint of animals, when children are encouraged to bring along their dogs, cats, donkeys, ponies, canaries, to be blessed in church. It is a touching scene, this procession of children, boys and girls with their fathers and mothers all dressed in their best. Behind children riding ponies, or carrying small dogs, tractors pull trailers loaded with goats and sheep, bales of straw and the occasional rabbit. I guess when times were really tough and animals essential to the survival of a farming family this feast was a genuine thanksgiving. No matter how hard I try I can't shake off the way abandoned animals are actually treated here; something, I'm afraid, which follows me around.

A House in the High Hills

Next morning Kendi and I are outside the bar in the sun, having a tisane, a tea made from fresh herbs which Pepita keeps in a glass jar behind the bar. Kendi has her nose in the dust, and most of the tables are full. The clock strikes eleven. A car comes down the hill towards us, going quite fast but slows as it nears and the window is wound down. A man in the passenger seat throws something into the square and revs off. Soon a plaintive wail comes from behind the hibiscus pot outside the restaurant and a small ginger cat runs for cover. It manages to get into the vestibule of the next house but the inner door is closed and now the kitten is frantic, scratching and clawing, desperate to be let in. Not one person outside the bar bothers. For a moment I wonder if this kitten actually belongs to the people who live in the house but its terrified yowls leave me in no doubt. As no one else seems willing to do anything, I have to go over and pick up the creature. Its little heart is pounding. What on earth am I going to do now?

When I ask if anyone enjoying their coffee on this sunny day will take the kitten because I have to leave the island in a couple of days, no one wants to know. So, the morning spoiled, Kendi and I take the kitten now purring in the palm of my hand back to the house and begin the forlorn task of phoning everyone I know. All of whom have cats. One has seven and another is feeding twenty. She's the one who suggests if I can't look after the cat myself I'll have to put it to sleep. It will be kinder all round, she says. Which is just great, as the kitten makes itself at home in an easy chair intending to stay for ever. In desperation I phone the animal sanctuary in Palma and get Isobel from Santa Ponsa on the line. She is sorry, she says, but they've been forced out of Palma and are trying to set up a new shelter near the airport. They can't take any more strays right now but she'll ring round her helpers and see if there is anything anyone can do. So many cats get dumped like this, she commiserates. I tell her she is literally my last resort.

That night I have a perfect little guest who knows how to use a litter tray, and sleeps through the night without a squeak. This is getting heavy. I am now down to wondering how I can smuggle him (being ginger it was, of course, a boy) in my hand luggage and take him with me when a truck rolls up and out get Isobel and Rebecca, thank God, carrying a cat box. 'Now don't you worry,' says Isobel, taking the kitten, 'One of our ladies is a cat lover and has five cats of her own but says one more won't make any difference. This lucky kitten is going to a happy home.'

I know it shouldn't be like this but when I finally make the plane to fly back to the UK having deposited Kendi at Nico's, I feel so enormously relieved I fall fast asleep and don't wake up until we're touching down at Heathrow.

eleven

I'm leaning into the sea wall and the wind is blowing strong from the south, churning the waves, throwing salt spray in my face. It is wild and refreshing, unusually so. This stretch of coast is usually filled with holidaymakers enjoying the sun but today there are only a few walking on what remains of a beach, most of which has disappeared in the winter storms. The undertow of the sea has exposed boulders and driftwood and gouged out a channel where the *torrente* runs, discharging rain water in rivulets. It could be any beach in winter, but this is Easter in the Mediterranean and soon more sand will need to be brought in, brushed and combed and sectioned ready for the summer's sun beds and thatched umbrellas.

I've come here because there's an all-day party in the castle on the hill and it's getting crowded. It's a special fiesta, one the locals look forward to each year because it is in a beautiful place, in the courtyard of the old fort, built originally to repel bandits but now an inviting setting for a spectacular picnic in Easter Week. I'm pleased to see Mario has arrived with his new girlfriend, Elena from the *colmada*. She'll keep him right.

In spite of the activity up at the castle, I'm managing, in this idyllic spot, to focus on what I must do next. I've already made the decision to close the house and return to Britain, feeling now is the time to get back into harness and quell my restlessness, although the prospect of leaving is sad. I came to this place to escape and already the handsome black cat who lives under the lentisk bush on the sea front has arrived, purring and pressing against me. She is an old friend. I have known her pretty much the whole time I've been on the island, bringing her water when it's hot, amazed at how smart she is, weaving through the crowds on the beach in high summer to find me. She's survived the culls and the closing of the cafés in the winter because she hangs around the only bar open all the year, so her being here now is surely a sign of good luck.

Kendi is enjoying the waves, barking as they crash and catch her paws, still not convinced having wet feet is part of the deal, but she's wearing away energy and that can only be good. I haven't been here long and the sharp sunshine is stinging. I'll get burned if I'm not careful so, soon, we reluctantly say goodbye to the beautiful cat and leave.

On the cusp of a hill, on the way out of San Telm is a simple, whitewashed cemetery. It lies on the southern edge of the bowl of the valley just before the winding road tips over and down to the village so I often have to pass it although it's a place I rarely visit. It is not at all gloomy but it's a sombre reminder of something I prefer not to have cloud my days. Today, however, as it's Easter Week and the people of the village are in my thoughts, I'm drawn to it.

The cemetery stands alone, its high stone wall framed by a thicket of wild olives and pines, so it's peculiarly quiet and has its own carved stone well. Thick wooden doors, which are never locked, open on to a sunlit arena, like a Roman amphitheatre, where all round sit the boxes of the dead. The oldest tombs are on the left, family graves carved to form a wall of golden stone whose sarcophagi, like large letter boxes, open at the front.

There is no avoiding the inscriptions on these tombs. They're stacked one on top of the other, four high, etched in a nineteenth-century flowery hand marking the names, the date of death and the age of those deposited here.

Each column of tombs is crowned with a gabled roof and a stone cross. Immediately next to these four are four more, then another four, and another, the remains and memories of those who have lived and worked in the village over the last one hundred years. Vich, Flexas, Porcell, Pujol, Alemany, the names recur as the men and women inscribed on the stone keep their mother's names along with their father's. Here the

story of the village is told. A close-knit community burgeoning into something stranger as the remains of different people
with different backgrounds begin to be interred here. The new
names, however, are in the main segregated from the old.
They have been put in their own enclosure to the north, a
chillier less ornate remembering.

Under one of the crosses in the main cemetery it says
'Familia de Baltasa Porcell', the family grave of Balthazar
Porcell. Other stone inscriptions, nearby, mark the demise of
other local characters with biblical names, Angel, Gabriel and
Jesus. Along with their age sometimes their relationship
to one another is recorded, a brother, a wife or a husband.
Nowhere does it say what they died of.

Almost every tomb has an oval enamelled photograph of
its inhabitant mounted on the front, which is a good idea. The
men, it seems, are serious, their wives serene. Most are in their
seventies and eighties, dressed in their Sunday best, their hair
combed as if to say look where we've ended up, look what
we've achieved.

Occasionally an exotic note disturbs the roll call of unaffected rural names. A colonel awarded the Chevalier de la
Legion d'Honneur, we know not why, lies three down from
the top in one of the older drawers. Unfortunately there is no
photo of him.

You have to walk past the old men and their moustaches
to get to the new burial site. Here they've economised on
space, digging down to make an extra tomb underground and

taking off the stone crosses to make way for another grave higher up. These are more filing cabinets than gothic hidey-holes, one of which has 'Bob' laid to rest inside. In felt-tipped pen someone has scrawled 'we luv ya Bob' across the front.

I'm not sure if Bob is in fact still in there. After some time the desiccated remains are scraped out, ready for the next laying-in.

If ever there's a need to find out who's died recently in the village it can be seen all too clearly here. Mateo, José and Juan, the three old friends of Sancho's, are all in residence, sadly; they must have passed away within months of one another. Their photos are up to date because they're wearing their favourite baseball caps. What upsets and surprises me most is Rafa. The young builder who looked like a conqueror must have died and I hadn't heard. He has his head cocked to one side, his inscription says he was only in his thirties. I wish I knew what had happened to him.

There is a day in Spain that remembers the dead more than any other. All Saints' Day on 1 November is also known as Todos los Santos, or the Day of the Dead. It is an important public holiday when people come with flowers and candles to give their 'ofrendas', offerings to the departed, usually almond cakes and flowers. The roads are packed with cars. This is the day when souls apparently find it easier to visit the living and so the local markets overflow with gladioli and lilies which end up in cemeteries like this all over the island. It's easy to forget sometimes that Spain is a Catholic country except on this day when whole families congregate in cemeteries to tend graves and tell stories about their loved ones. Today the cemetery is peaceful, the only sound, birds singing in the trees and I'm glad I've come here to complete the circle, to be reacquainted with those I feel I knew.

The forest framing the cemetery is where the fire blazed. A small path goes from here up into the hills where the scorched earth is now greening. The burned trees, which once stood skeletal against the sky, are softened with wild broom and flowers, almost as if the fire never happened. Already young pine trees are shooting up so that in a few years the slopes will be forested again and the walls and old paths submerged from view. Kendi loves walking here mainly because there's no one around and she can gallop freely in the direction of my house. She now knows her way home.

It's been a sombre walk but I have a message waiting for me which is about to change Kendi's life. Someone called Robert Winsor wants me to call. He's been reading about Kendi in the local paper and has left his telephone number. Kendi and I turned up at a charity fete on one of my 'socialising Kendi' excursions and had our photo taken. I'd mentioned I was looking for a home for her.

On the phone Robert Winsor tells me he devotes his time raising money for underprivileged children in Mallorca but he knows a woman who he believes may be able to help me with Kendi. 'She's called Glenda,' he says, 'Glenda Dean, and I will introduce you if you can come to Santa Ponsa on Saturday.'

Santa Ponsa, again. I wonder if Glenda Dean is a member of the Ladies' Club. Either way I can hardly wait to see her.

It takes me a while to find her. Her secluded house, tucked into a hillside of pine trees, is reached by a long paved drive flanked with showered lawns, banana trees and palms, like one you'd find in Miami Beach. Two Great Danes, gentle dogs that come up to my shoulder, greet me sedately, paddling off to find their mistress, swaying and sashaying slowly towards the sound of voices coming from under a gazebo in the garden, taking their time, unwilling to do anything so common as hurry, like a couple of flunkies on dope. If Kendi came to live here she'd bustle these two along.

Robert and Glenda are having cocktails by the pool. Robert is wearing gold and seems to be a bit of a dynamo with his multifarious interests and deserving charities. Glenda is a glamorous Miss Moneypenny, blonde and tanned and savvy, a woman who ran her own public relations firm for big City dealers before selling up to live a luxurious life in the sun. If high finance is her background, her passion, I'm about to discover, is dogs and their welfare. After pressing a Bloody Mary on me Glenda comes straight out with her offer. She wants to give Kendi a lift back to Britain. She has a plane, a private plane, so Kendi can walk straight on and off with no hold-ups and no hold.

The Bloody Mary has suddenly become the best I have ever tasted.

'Do you mean that?' I cannot believe what I'm hearing. I'd

been coming round to thinking how Kendi might enjoy living in Santa Ponsa after all and now this.

Glenda is matter of fact. 'Of course. I hate the idea of any dog being put through hell in the hold of a plane. I once had to do it with one of mine and I don't know who was more stressed at the end of the flight, me or it. Never again.'

I want to say I haven't given any thought to Kendi coming back to the UK, that I want her to stay on the island, but how churlish is that going to sound when here is someone prepared to make the major obstacle, the journey back to Britain, as easy as boarding a bus: no forcing Kendi into a cage, no delays, no horrendous noise and confusion, just turn up and hop on. I feel elated and anxious all at once.

Glenda is brisk. 'You must come and meet the gang,' she says.

'Gang?'

'Yes, there's a group of us who get together to raise money for the Calvia refuge. I want you to meet Martha and her husband who are full of fun and will help you get Kendi's passport sorted out. We're having lunch at the club today with my husband, Stephen, you must come along.'

I've left Kendi in the car, not sure how she'd cope in a posh house with its posh dogs, but Glenda insists that she wants to meet her and walks me up the drive with the two Great Danes, Robert and a rescue spaniel who's appeared from behind a pot of geraniums. I'm getting nervous because Kendi may feel threatened and growl. I don't want her to blow her one opportunity of getting out of here.

Glenda, however, is not fazed. 'Isn't she lovely?' she enthuses as Kendi leaps at the window, baring her teeth. The Great Danes aren't a bit perturbed either, but I'm not for risking an encounter just now. 'I'll set off to the club,' I offer, a bit too hurriedly, 'and give Kendi a quick walk before lunch. See you there.'

A scrawny and unkempt Kendi slinks into the back seat as Glenda's sleek hounds amble back to the pool while I make a mental note that my dog is definitely going to have to smarten up if she's being invited to fly private.

Lunch is outside on the patio of the Santa Ponsa Club overlooking the rolling golf course with me, Glenda, Martha and their husbands, Stephen and Mark. It is lovely to relax with the sun on my back. Everyone is supportive, assuring me they're up for this bushtucker trial which will see Kendi, apparently a celebrity on the island, out of here fast. The pity is, if she had been going to Germany she'd be there by now. Britain has a double dose of rabies tests; Germany has just the one. If a dog is rabies free and has the antibodies, there is no hindrance to it flying. This probably explains why so many strays find their way to Germany from Mallorca. It's easier to get them there. Kendi has to have several more tests and injections before they'll let her out.

Martha is tall, assertive and expressive, she is one of those Englishwomen made of steel girders who lives practically permanently in Mallorca. Like Glenda, she doesn't believe in messing around and the mention of councillors in Calvia gets her fizzing. It gets them both fizzing. Martha's taken on the Calvia council over strays and engineered fund-raising to support a happier solution to the problem, backing the local sanctuary, but she's up against it.

Over a lunch of sole and lobster, Martha tells me Glenda has raised a staggering amount of money in a one-day golf tournament, which is supposed to go to the refuge but Calvia council refuses to give permission for it to happen. It's the same old story. Like the other refuge in Palma, the women who work their socks off for the animals don't want to offend those with the power to shut them down. It's a sad state of affairs in a country signed up to enthusiastic clubbiness in Europe.

Martha says anything she can do to help she will. If I need her to check on Kendi, while she is with Nico, she will. So on this cheerful note we get down to setting the dates of our departure. Before I go, I promise to check in with Glenda again when I have all the paperwork.

Kendi is sick on the way back. It's all too much for her and I'm seriously concerned about how she is going to manage the thousand-mile journey by plane if she can't cope with a titchy trip in a car. Kendi's car sickness has been a problem from the beginning, but I tell myself to be a bit more like Glenda and cool down. If she isn't hyped then neither should I be. What's more important is my coming to terms with having Kendi for ever. If this trip comes off then Kendi's new home will be very different from the one she is used to. It will be cold and windy and wild. Her paws will be wet more often than dry. I daren't contemplate how she's going to be able to adapt, particularly as she's not a puppy. Anything, however, can happen before then.

The next morning, as the sun lights up the valley I discover, under the olive trees in the field, a wedge of wild artichokes shielded deep in luxuriant foliage, ready to pick. I fetch a basket and knife and trim away. Soon I have a gift of eight purple artichokes to take to a friend who has invited Kendi and me to supper. Gina and her husband Tommy have a fabulous house in the mountains of Mallorca and as Gina has already gone through hell to bring back a poor dog she found lost in Greece, she knows I need my confidence building.

'Now she's going to be an international traveller,' she had enthused over the phone when I tell her we've both got a lift back to the UK. 'Kendi needs to learn a few manners.'

———

A couple of days later I'm cruising with a car-sick Kendi round the tight bends in the centre of the island, leading to Gina and Tommy's hilltop retreat. Coveys of partridge whirr into the setting sun as we turn off the road and everywhere, it seems, is wilderness. Hares weave in front of us, slowing us, as the single-track road makes for lights in the distance and a courtyard where Tommy is waiting. Kendi is wearing a new blue collar for the occasion, but even so she still looks like a bedraggled wolf with her nibbled ears and unfortunately begins to behave like one.

'Don't worry, don't worry,' says Tommy as Kendi gets out of the car in a crouch, trying to find an escape route. Gina has appeared and is not having any of this nonsense. She soothes Kendi and leads her gently into a glamorous room full of soft sofas and low lights where a log fire and Helen and Kiki, friends of Gina and Tommy's, are there to greet us. Unfortunately they've also brought their three effervescent black-and-white spaniels. I can feel my heart speeding as Kendi sets off on a circuit of these well-behaved folk, rangily rounding up her prey. She's never seen a gathering like it. There's some growling and one of the spaniels, a female, lurches at Kendi. The silky conversation is suddenly torn. This is Gina's moment. In her lovely home with its luxurious furnishing she's not a bit fussed, focusing instead on a poor dog, overwhelmed. She knows what Kendi needs, reassurance, and she's there to give it her. Stroking Kendi tenderly, Gina coaxes and tells her how welcome she is and soon Kendi relaxes on the rug, happy to have found such a good friend in this strange new place.

For a dog whose whole life has been the confines of a dirty kennel it can't get more surreal than this. Here dinner is served with silver cutlery by candlelight. A table laid with a pristine damask cloth drapes down, an inch above the floor at nose level. Soon food will appear which smells divine. Kendi has never encountered the likes of it but reckons lurking amongst all these expensive toes in the folds of the damask cloth might be her best bet. I pray she won't disgrace me.

As the conversation turns to the political shenanigans on the island Kendi begins to grumble. A low mumble at first, and then a full-blown growl emanates from near my feet. A spaniel has crawled under the cloth to check out Kendi and Kendi is not having it. There's a snarling and something belts out into the sitting room, it's black and white so it's not Kendi, and the conversation dips and picks up again.

By the time we've finished eating I'm ragged. All I want is to make the best exit I can with a dog that's turned as nervy as me but Gina is determined Kendi has come all this way and has to have supper. 'She is so thin,' she says. So her cook brings a fine plate of steak, chopped, which she places before Kendi in the corner of the room. In a second, in a couple of gulps, the lot's gone, and Kendi looks up as though to say, this is more like it. She's now, of course, not for leaving. Over camomile tea in the drawing room Kendi makes herself at home, crashing out, eyes closed tight on the rug near the fire. When it's finally long past our bedtime and she can't hang back any longer with her new best friends, the spaniels by the fire, she reluctantly musters a well-mannered goodbye, eases herself into the space under the dashboard and sinks into a deep sleep of exhaustion, as I navigate our way home. For the first time ever she's not a bit car sick.

After this my confidence in what is to become my dog for good grows daily. Gina phones to say how adorable Kendi is and altogether I feel a little less anxious about the future if someone as discerning as Gina can see the potential in her.

My leaving the island coincides, for the first time, with there being no dramas in the valley. Lauren is back and picking up her life and I've asked Nico to caretake my house while I am away. He says he will enjoy walking up daily to check on things and will keep the garden tidy and the pool clean in spite of his physical disabilities. I think it will be good for him to work like this. I pray he doesn't go and get another dog. Gunther has become a farmer again and has one of the best vegetable plots in the district. Francine now smiles when she sees me and I reciprocate. There is even talk of the road being repaired, finally. As for Emmy Lou, well she is enjoying electricity after thirty years without, so there is much to keep everyone out of mischief.

———

On the day of our departure, it's windy and threatening rain. We're travelling light; I have a few essentials in a bag and a bottle of water for Kendi. She has had her last jab and has to be out of the country before it wears off, so very early, after closing the shutters and locking the door, we walk determinedly down to a taxi which will take us to Palma and the private air terminal to meet up with Glenda. We have a long, long journey ahead.